老子易知解

LAO-TZU:

"My words are very easy to understand."

Lectures on the
Tao Teh Ching
by
Man-jan Cheng

鄭曼髯註

Translated from the Chinese
by **Tam C. Gibbs**

NORTH ATLANTIC BOOKS, RICHMOND, CALIFORNIA

LAO-TZU: "MY WORDS ARE VERY EASY TO UNDERSTAND."
Lectures on the *Tao Teh Ching* by Man-jan Cheng

Published by: North Atlantic Books
2320 Blake Street
Berkeley, California 94704

Chinese edition published by:
Chung Hwa Book Company, Ltd.
94, Section 1, South Chungking Road,
Taipei, Taiwan, Republic of China
December, 1971

Cover and design by Paula Morrison

Typeset in Palatino by Joe Safdie

ISBN 0-913028-91-6

Lao-Tzu: "My Words Are Very Easy To Understand" is sponsored by the Society for the Study of Native Arts and Sciences, a nonprofit educational corporation whose goals are to develop an ecological and cross-cultural perspective linking various scientific, social, and artistic fields; to nurture a holistic view of arts, sciences, humanities, and healing; and to publish and distribute literature on the relationship of mind, body, and nature.

L. C. Catalog Card Number 82-241268

Contents

課老子感言 An Affectionate Word About the Class on Lao-tzu

Having recently completed *Lao-tzu: My Words Are Very Easy To Understand,* my students entreated me to teach them. Opening date for the class is August 15, 1970, and I have been moved by the occasion to address a few remarks to clarify my reasons for writing this book.

Lao-tzu wrote in the period following the *Six Classics* and preceeding the *Four Books,* so he was one of the earliest writers in Chinese history. His work describes the merest traces and indescribable marvels of the Tao and promotes Non-action, concepts which are central to these unique teachings of thousands of years ago.

Over the past 2,400 years and more, approximately 1,400 people have offered interpretations of Lao-tzu. Of the extant 700 or so interpretations, the Englishman Arthur Waley had the gall to comment that none plumb to the heart of Lao-tzu. Regrettably, Waley's own interpretation is only superficial. Therefore I feel constrained to speak up and make my views known.

Lao-tzu himself says, "my words are very easy to understand." How is it then that even after more than a thousand expert commentaries we are still in suspense? The commentaries of the Han Dynasty, from Ho-shang Kung (fl. 179-159 B.C.), to Yen Chün-p'ing (a.k.a. Yen Tsun, fl. 53-24 B.C.), to Ko Hsüan (fl. 210 A.D.), are comparatively appropriate. Then came Wang Pi (226-249 A.D.), who ignores the opinions of his predecessors and diverges from the meaning of the text. Ever since the T'ang and Sung Dynasties, each scholar has had his own interpretation, transforming Lao-tzu into a million different shapes. Nine out of ten researchers invoke Chuang-tzu as the prime source on Lao-tzu. But Chuang-tzu communicates through fables; how can we follow his footprints to find Lao-tzu?

Because of the vast differences between ancient and modern Chinese, the Han Dynasty commentaries on semantics are most useful. One can sort through systematic commentaries, from Ho-shang Kung to Wang Pi, and select the cogent ones. One also ought to listen to the varied and contrasting theories. If sense and meaning collide, be content to suspend judgment.

Although Lao-tzu was a profoundly practical man, human emotions disgusted him greatly, and he longed to get away. He hoped for a new beginning through metamorphosis, or, as the phrase has it, "his step leaves no footprint." How much more difficult it is to find the tracks of Lao-tzu's mind! Only one man understood, and that was Confucius. Did he not say Lao-tzu was like a dragon? How right he was! How can any flying or walking creature compare with dragon-like Lao-tzu?

Hence, in making this *Lao-tzu: My Words Are Very Easy to Understand*, I have focused on Lao-tzu's "my words have their sources, my deeds their precedents." For instance, "through Non-action there is nothing left undone," also means that through Non-desire there is nothing left undesired. Hence, "use the orthodox to govern a nation; use the unorthodox to wage war," "governing a large country is like frying a small fish," and "do nothing and yet win the world," illustrate that the orthodox can turn into the unorthodox. The unorthodox finally returns to Non-action, even to the traces and marvels at the gateway to Lao-tzu's Tao.

To put it simply, the secret is all in Lao-tzu's esoteric magic. Can we really practice it or not? I am afraid we can only wait and see.

Whiskers Man
New York City

易知解，而專從老子之言有宗，事有君，體會得之。如其所謂無爲而無不爲，亦可謂無欲而無不欲。故謂以正治國，以奇用兵，治大國若烹小鮮，以無事而取天下。可見正復爲奇，奇仍歸乎無事。至於徼妙乃老子之門道，簡直言之，即其秘密之訣竅也，其易行歟否？恐猶有待乎來者。

己酉處暑曼髯寫於紐約

An Affectionate Word About the Class on Lao-tzu

致有隔閡。惟河上之言，較平允，至晉王弼，乃抹煞前人之說，則離矣！唐宋以來人各異說。使老子化身遂成千億，考之者十九援莊子以爲證，莊生寓言以寄意，何可泥其跡也。若論字義之訓詁，古今文固大異，漢之諸賢，却已論定，如河上及王弼諸家本，可酌從者從之，議之者，雖紛紜，聽之可耳。倘意與義乖。闕疑爲愈，雖然老子蓋深於世故者，乃甚厭人情。而欲肥遯，希有蟬脫塵埃之舉。故謂夫跡有非履之喻，而況以跡求老氏之心者乎？知之者惟仲尼一人而已。謂老子其猶龍乎？信矣。然老子既猶龍然，安可取飛與走者爲喻？故予爲老子

課老子感言

近著有老子易知解，諸生乞予授之，茲定於中秋開課，感述數言，聊以見意。老子之作，後六經而先四書，乃最古之作家也。崇尚微妙，以鼓吹無爲，可謂成千古獨特之言。垂二千四百餘年，注釋者達千四百人，現存幾七百家，英人威壘，敢大膽譏評，謂俱未得老氏之心有以也。惜威壘氏之注，亦僅奏膚功，故予猶未能已乎言者，以有所見也。老子自謂，吾言最易知，何以注逾千家，猶爲懸解。漢自河上公、嚴君平、葛玄諸人之注，俱泥道家語，

卷頭小引 A Short Introduction

Tao: There are three kinds of Tao. The *Ten Wings* of the *Book of Change* says, "the Tao of heaven is built upon *yin* and *yang*; the Tao of earth is based on the soft and hard; the Tao of mankind stands on humanism and justice." Put simply, Tao is a path, a way of thinking.

What Lao-tzu Calls Tao: Differing greatly from Confucius, Lao-tzu borrows the changes and cycles of *yin* and *yang* and the soft and the hard to construct the Tao of heaven and earth or Nature. He champions Non-action and opposes the Tao of humanism and justice which man stands upon as a foundation. He believed that conscious action was not beautiful. Only that which Confucius spoke of as humanism and justice pave the orthodox road for mankind to follow.

Principles of Wisdom: The *Book of Documents* says, "the wise possess enduring Teh." The phrase means those who grasp enduring *Teh* realize wisdom. Wisdom and sagacity are complementary: sagacity aids Tao in creation, while wisdom aids the fecundity of Teh. Sagacity is an ideal, wisdom is a reality. Confucius would not accept the title of sage. When on the verge of death he said of himself, "the wise man is withering away."

The common translation of Principles of Wisdom *(che-li)* as "philosophy" is mistaken. The "study of knowledge" is too broad to describe either Lao-tzu's "by Non-action embrace the One" or Confucius' "my Tao is strung on a single thread." These are Principles of Wisdom.

Tao Teh Ching: The *Book of Change* says, "Tao is the aid heaven gives to the origin of things; Teh is the aid earth gives to the growth process." Tao and Teh, then, is simply the Tao of heaven and the Teh of earth. *Ching* means "constant, everyday" *(ch'ang).* Thus that which is "classic" is the constancy of Tao.

A Short Introduction

哲理

書稱經德秉哲，經常也，卽謂常德所秉持者，哲之實也。哲與聖相較，聖猶資始之道，哲猶資生之德，亦卽聖猶名也，哲猶實也。故夫聖，孔子不居，及其臨沒，則自謂哲人其萎。近世翻譯弗羅索非爲哲學，錯了！弗羅索非，乃廣義之智學，非老子所謂無爲抱一，孔子所謂吾道一以貫之之哲理也。

道德經

易曰：天之資始道也，地之資生德也。所謂道德者，卽天地之道德也。經者常也。卽所謂經者，道之常也。

卷頭小引

道

道有三，易繫辭曰，立天之道，曰陰與陽，立地之道，曰柔與剛，立人之道，曰仁與義。淺近言之，道譬猶道路也。然此路，係屬於思路，則有以異乎道路也。

老子之所謂道

與孔子大異，老子假陰陽剛柔之變化與推移，乃天地自然之道。爲鼓吹無爲之說，反立人曰仁與義之道，以爲有爲而不美。惟孔子之謂仁與義，正猶人所應由之道路耳。

老聃傳 Biography of Lao Tan

Lao-tzu's surname was Lao and his given name was Tan. He was from Hsiang in the state of Ch'en.[1] Non-action and Non-name are vital elements of his Tao and Teh. Recently Yen Ling-feng, in researching appropriate antecedents, said that during the Spring and Autumn period the surname Li (里) was scarce. There was a Li K'e in the state of Chin,[2] a Li Ke in the state of Lu,[3] and no occurence of the surname Lee (李). The surname Lao originated with the son of Chuan Hsu,[4] Lao T'ung. After him, the *Compendium of Customs and Usages*[5] mentions Lao-tzu as having the same family name. It becomes apparent that the information given by Ssu-ma Ch'ien is not reliable: he was the real cause behind the Lee family taking Lao Tan as their first ancestor, thus cutting off the ancestral sacrifices of the Lao family.

Lao Tan never was an ordinary person. Did not Confucius once say he was like a dragon? How true those words were!

As for government, Lao-tzu reaches for positive results through negative methods, hence "governing a great nation is like cooking a small fish." His military tactics uses the weaker to overcome the stronger as a rider controls his galloping steed, and the insubstantial to penetrate where there is no opening. He speaks of using the orthodox to govern a nation and the unorthodox to fight a war.

Ultimately, this course of Non-action brings about "traces and marvels." Learning is to learn Non-learning. Lao-tzu even goes to the point of desiring Non-desire. Learning that one can learn is not everlasting learning; desire that one can desire is not everlasting desire.

Then what does he mean by "everlasting learning" and "everlasting desire?" Know the masculine, cleave to the feminine; know the hard, cleave to the soft; know the strong, cleave to the gentle; know glory, cleave to humility; know the advance, cleave to retreat; know what is, cleave to what is not.

To be wrapped by *yin* and contain *yang* means to be enclosed by the exterior, yet know the *yin;* and to be contained within the interior, yet know the *yang*. To *"contain yang"* means inhaling the *ch'i* of heaven; to be "wrapped by *yin*" means transforming spermic essence *(ching)* into bone marrow. The marrow flows inside the bones and the *ch'i* circulates throughout—even to the feet—with the breath. When one arrives at this level, one's "pulsing *ch'i*s marry." The realization of this is called "diffusing glare, uniting with the world." This is what Lao-tzu desires, this is what to study: the marriage of the *ch'i* is Tao or the province of men who are in communication with heaven. How then could Lao-tzu not have hoped that someone would practice it.

Lao-tzu was an officer of the Chou government in charge of the imperial library. He held the post for a long time, remaining in obscurity. Frustrated that his Tao was not being practiced, he quit his post and went to a frontier pass. A man named Hsi who was in charge of the pass said, "Sir, you will be going into seclusion. Force yourself to to write us a book." Thereupon Lao-tzu wrote five thousand characters on Tao and Teh and then went on his way. No one knows what happened to him.

The first time Confucius traveled to the capital of Chou, he went to ask Lao-tzu about Tao. When Confucius' words touched on humanism and justice, Lao-tzu said, "What you, sir, have spoken of today is like a footprint. That which made the footprint has gone, and how, alas, can the print be taken for the foot?" He also said, "If the time is ripe, a ruler can take the reins; if it is not ripe, he must pack up and be off. I have heard that the peddler of quality hides valuable items at the bottom of his pack and appears to have nothing; the ruler of quality appears foolish. Rid yourself, sir, of your arrogant air and myriad desires. None of them are the least bit good for you, sir. I would say to you, sir, nothing more than that." When Confucius left, Lao-tzu saw him off, saying, "I have heard that men of wealth and position give presents of money when seeing someone off, while men of culture give words of advice. I cannot be considered a man of wealth or position, so I will appropriate the status of man of culture and present you, sir, with a word of advice: Widely informed men and gifted orators endanger themselves by inviting the hatred of others. Children have no self; officials have no self." At the time, Confucius was not yet fifty years old. How could he be worthy of Lao-tzu's admonishments if not for his abundant virtue (Teh)? Would not Lao-tzu, as champion of natural transformation through Non-action, normally be loathe to utter so many words?

The men who followed Confucius did not respect Lao-tzu and believed his alleged advice was worthless. The followers of Lao-tzu did not respect Confucius, and felt compelled to prove the validity of Lao-tzu's words. The whole situation became quite laughable.

Lao-tzu definitely wanted to practice his words, but the time was not ripe, and so he had to pack up and be off. Confucius also had ambitions he wanted to realize, saying, "I am a driver!" To the end of his days, Confucius used Tao to "chauffeur" men. Lao-tzu seems to have mounted a dragon and ascended to heaven. Let each practice his Tao and leave it at that. What is the purpose of each attacking the other? In what way are they mutually exclusive?

Whiskers Man Cheng
New York City
May 19, 1967

Notes

1. Situated in what is now central Honan.
2. Occupying parts of today's Shansi and Hopei provinces.
3. Present day Shantung province.
4. A ruler of China, 2513-2435 B.C.
5. *Feng-ssu T'ung-yi,* a book explaining ancient customs and mores written in the Han dynasty.

Biography of Lao Tan

爲人臣者，毋以有已。當是時也，孔子年不過强仕
，固能得老氏之箴言若是，若非以其有盛德也，老
子以無爲自化者，惡肯出此言也？後之學儒者，則
絀老，以爲所言未足信；學老者，亦絀儒；必欲實
是言也，俱殊可笑，爲老氏者，却已實行其言矣。
不得其時，則蓬累而行。爲孔氏者，亦已實行其志
焉。曰：吾執御焉！孔子終其身，御人以道。老子
則猶乘風雲而上天，各行其道可耳。復何有相犯者
焉？又何有相背者焉？

丁未五月十九日寫於紐約

居之久，莫之知，而歎其道之不行，去之至關。關尹喜曰：子將隱，强爲我著書。廼述道德五千言而行，莫知所終。初孔子適周，往問道焉，語及仁義，老子曰：今子之所言，猶迹也，夫迹履之所出，而迹豈履哉。又曰：且君子得時則駕，不得其時，則蓬累而行。吾聞之良賈，深藏若虛，君子盛德，容貌若愚，去子之驕氣與多欲，是皆無益於子之身，吾所以告子，若是而已。孔子辭，而老子送之曰：吾聞富貴者，送人以財，仁人者，送人以言，吾不能富貴，竊仁人之號，送子以言曰：博辯廣大，危其身者，發人之惡者也。爲人子者，毋以有己。

無間，故謂以正治國，以奇用兵，極其所謂微妙者，爲無爲已耳。觀其所爲學，則謂學不學，以及乎欲不欲，亦卽猶學可學，非常學，欲可欲，非常欲也。究其所謂常學常欲者，何也？知其雄，守其雌，知其剛，守其柔，以及知壯守弱，知榮守辱，知進守退，知有守無之類，此之謂負陰而抱陽，負形於外，守其陰也，抱容於內，知其陽也。抱陽者，服天氣也，負陰者，化精髓也，髓行骨中，氣循踵息，得其用者，冲氣以爲和耳。是之謂和其光，而同其塵，此老氏之欲之學，合而之謂道。亦可謂通天人之際，豈不欲有以行之哉？爲周守藏室之史，

老聃傳

鄭曼髯

老子者，姓老名聃，陳國相人也，修道德，以無爲無名爲務。近有嚴氏靈峯，考之當理，謂春秋時僅有姓里，晉有里克，魯有里革，而無李姓者。老氏蓋出於顓頊之子，老童之後，見風俗通義與老萊子乃同姓耳。始知司馬遷之說，不可從也。李宗之子孫，以聃爲初祖，而老氏之祀遂絕，遷實使之然也。聃固非常人，孔子嘗稱其猶龍邪？信哉斯言。老氏之言政也，寓積極於消極之中，故所謂治大國若烹小鮮。其言兵也，以至柔馳騁至堅，以無有而入

上篇 Part 1

一章 Chapter 1

The tao that can be said is not the everlasting Tao.

Lecture: That which can be categorized and classified is not the everlasting and immutable Tao of Nature.

If a name can be named, it is not the everlasting Name.

"Tao is always without a name," and "tao" is not actually the "everlasting and immutable Name" of heaven and earth which participated in the beginnings and growth of the myriad things.

That which has no name is the origin of heaven and earth;
That which has a name is the Mother of all things.

"That which has no name" and "that which has a name" are explained elsewhere in the text in this fashion: "something is born of nothing." Once the world begins existing it becomes the Mother. After the Mother exists, she gives birth to the myriad things. This process of birth is elsewhere called Mysterious Female, the root of heaven and earth. In Chapter 32 it says, "the Tao is always without a name," and further on in the same chapter, "at the genesis of the world name came into being." All the above are continuations of a single idea.

Thus, if always without desire, one can observe
indescribable marvels;
If always desirous, one sees merest traces.
Those two come from the same source but are differently named.
Both are called Mysterious.
The mystery of the Mysterious is the gateway
to all indescribable marvels.

"Merest traces" is a lesser path *(tao)*. "Merest traces" and "indescribable marvels" come from the same source but with different names. Then the text says, "both are called Mysterious," and finishes with, "the gateway to all indescribable marvels." In clarification, "indescribable marvels" provide a gateway to the Tao; "merest traces" provide a side-path. Further on the text states, "the door of the Mysterious Female is called the root of heaven and earth," and, "in opening and closing heaven's gate, can you do it without the Female?" These references are all explanations of what is called the Mother of the myriad things. In dealing with the most important precepts of Lao-tzu, Non-action and Non-desire, what can be made of the sudden assertion, "if always desirous, one sees merest traces?" If taken together with the words in Chapter 64, "the Sage desires Non-desire," one will begin to understand the "desire" of the Sage as explained, using Lao-tzu's style: the desire that can be desired is not everlasting Desire.

Note: The eternal Tao and the everlasting Name are not compatible with the Tao of Man as described by Confucius: humanism and justice. What Lao-tzu calls the eternal Tao of Nature focuses specifically on *Yin* and *Yang,* soft and hard. In particular, he emphasizes that *Yin* conquers *Yang,* soft overcomes hard. His intense dislike of action as implicit in the Tao of Mankind leads to the statement "action is false" and therefore he champions Non-action. In another place Lao-tzu says, "everlasting Non-desire can be called the lesser. That all things return to (the Tao) and yet (the Tao) does not act as their master can be called the greater." In short, the everlasting Name is just this: (the eternal Tao of Nature). The lines, "observe the indescribable marvels . . . see the merest traces. Those two come from the same source but are differently named," provide a gateway to the Tao; they are two (duality) and yet one (unity).

Chapter 1

。同出而異名。同謂之玄。玄之又玄。衆妙之門。

徼小道也。徼與妙，同出而異名，同謂之玄，故結之曰：衆妙之門。是明說，妙有門，徼有道也。下文又曰：玄牝之門，爲天地根。又曰：天門開闔能無雌乎，悉謂萬物之母，之注解耳。然老子之所尙，乃無爲無欲，忽又謂：常有欲，以觀其徼何也？必合六十四章，謂是以聖人欲不欲，並觀之，始可知聖人之欲，亦猶欲可欲，乃非常欲之意已耳。

按所謂常道常名者，乃非仁義之人道。而老子獨取陰陽剛柔，稱天地之常道，而尤詡陰以勝陽，柔以勝剛，嫌人道以有爲，爲僞故鼓吹無爲，又謂常無欲可名於小，萬物歸焉而不爲主，可名爲大。所謂常名者，如是而已。且觀妙觀徼，乃同出而異名，其爲門道者，二而一也。（按者，竊以我見而分析之，以下同此不贅。）

一章

道可道。非常道。

道，可以稱道之者，非天地常久不滅之道。

名可名。非常名。

道常無名，如可稱道之者，乃非資始資生、如天地常久不滅之名。

無名天地之始。有名萬物之母。

無名有名，下文已自解曰：有生於無，天下有始，以爲天下母。有母然後生萬物，此之謂元牝，爲天地根。且三十二章有謂，道常無名，又曰：始制有名。皆是承此意耳。

故常無欲。以觀其妙。常有欲。以觀其徼。此兩者

二章 Chapter 2

If everyone understands the beautiful as beauty,
It is ugly.
If everyone understands goodness as good,
It is not good at all.

Lecture: Compare these lines with those elsewhere: "the fewer who know me, the more valuable I am." This is the paradox of the mutual support of opposites; beauty and goodness become meaningless when everyone acknowledges them.

Note: I myself hold that humanism is the most beautiful of all things, and that justice is the greatest good of all. Lao-tzu's point of view is not only contrary to this, he even says that beauty is abnormal. This, in fact and substance, takes the humanism and justice of the Confucian Tao of Mankind to be neither beautiful nor good.

Is and is not are mutually arising;
Difficult and easy are complementary;
Long and short arise from comparison;
Higher and lower are interdependent;
Vocalization and verbalization harmonize with each other;
Before and after accompany each other.

The foregoing six phrases describing mutual functions should be taken with the words of Chapter 27; "good people are examples for mediocre people, while mediocre people have the potential to be good people."

This is why the Sage manages affairs of Non-action and performs wordless teaching.
The myriad things are made without the slightest word.
[Nature] gives birth but does not possess.
It acts but does not demand subservience.
It is deserving of merit, yet claims no merit.
Only because it claims no credit is it indispensible.

In Chapter 25 it says, "man follows earth, earth follows heaven, heaven follows Tao, Tao follows Nature." This is the description of "gives birth but does not possess, acts but does not demand subservience," teaching to perform without waiting for words. The Yellow Emperor followed this doctrine.

Chapter 2

是以聖人處無爲之事。行不言之教。萬物作焉而不辭。生而不有。爲而不恃。功成而弗居。夫唯弗居。是以不去。

此卽廿五章人法地，地法天，天法道，道法自然，是爲生而不有，爲而不恃，教不待言而行，黃帝其由之焉。

二　章

天下皆知美之爲美。斯惡已。皆知善之爲善。斯不善已。

此與下文，知我者希，則我者貴，相反相承，可見皆知其爲美爲善者，亦以賤焉。

按仁爲天下之最美者，義爲天下之最善者。而老聃不獨有以反之，且謂善復爲妖，乃實以人道之仁義，爲不美不善矣。

故有無相生。難易相成。長短相較。高下相傾。音聲相和。前後相隨。

自難易以至前後，乃六句皆互相爲用，可與廿七章善人者不善人之師，不善人者善人之資，可並觀而得其趣矣。

三

章 Chapter 3

Not honoring men of worth keeps the people from competing;
Not wanting rare things keeps the people from thievery;
Not paying attention to the desirable keeps the hearts of the people from disaster.

Lecture: These are called the benefits of Non-action.

That is why the Sage governs himself by
relaxing the mind,
reinforcing the abdomen,
gentling the will,
strengthening the bones.

"Govern" means to regulate by certain principles. "Relaxing the mind" (lit. making the heart vacuous) is the doctrine of Non-action. "Reinforcing the abdomen" means, in the words of the Yellow Emperor: "the Sage swallows the Breath *(ch'i)* of heaven to reach spiritual enlightenment." In Chapter 20 it says, "prize the food of the Mother." 'Mother' is the mother of all living things, the life-giving 'Breath' *(ch'i)* of heaven-earth. This is the Tao of Lao-tzu. The will resides in the spleen ("gentling the will"). The bones ("strengthening the bones") are related to the urogenital system. The spleen is the root of post-natal life, and the urogenital system determines pre-natal life. Furthermore, the urogenital system governs one's strength. If one's will is too strong, it will not only harm one's primal energy, but will also harm the very root and trunk of one's life-span. How can one strengthen the bones? By cultivating the spermic essence *(ching)* and filling the bones with marrow as was taught by Ch'i-po, the teacher of the Yellow Emperor. Ch'i-po said, "strengthening of bone and marrow is the root of life itself." If one were to say that the way the Sage governs himself were no more than to fill the belly with food, how could Lao-tzu's *Tao Teh Ching* be worthy of its title?

Always cause the people to be without knowledge or desires;
Cause the intelligent ones to not dare act.
Let there be Non-action
And there is nothing that will not be well-regulated.

Chapter 65 reads, ". . . not to enlighten the people, but instead gradually (make) them stupid." Chapter 20 says, "What a fool's mind I have! How muddled I am!" Lao-tzu introduces this because he desires to gradually transform the people.

Translator's Note: According to the *Yellow Emperor's Classic on Internal Medicine,* the will resides in the spleen. The urogenital system (including the kidneys) is related to the bones. The spleen helps the stomach digest food.

The urogenital system, referred to as *hsien t'ien* (see below) in traditional Chinese medical terminology, relates directly to the strength of one's parents. Up until the time of birth, life is totally dependent on the strength of one's parents, and so it is called *hsien t'ien* or 'pre-heaven, which can also be translated as 'pre-natal.' According to Chinese medicine all the strength one has (eyesight, hearing, energy, taste, etc.) depends on the strength of the urogenital system.

The will is inversely related to the energy of the spleen. If the will is too strong, it draws energy from the spleen. If the spleen's energy is imbalanced, it will borrow energy from the urogenital system, diminishing one's basic energy. This is based upon the Five Elements system used in traditional Chinese medicine, that is, the spleen (earth) "overcomes" the urogenital system (water).

Ching is not just sperm or semen. It is the basic energy whereof sperm is made. The marrow of the bones is affected by the energy of this substance, according to Ch'i-po in the *Yellow Emperor's Classic on Internal Medicine.*

Chapter 3

食，亦足以爲老子之道德經乎？

常使民無知無欲。使夫智者不敢爲也。爲無爲則無不治。

六十五章謂：非以明民，將以愚之。此謂：我愚人之心也哉！沌沌兮老子將欲有以化民，故倡之。

三 章

不尚賢。使民不爭。不貴難得之貨。使民不爲盜。不見可欲。使民心不亂。

是稱無爲之利。

是以聖人之治。虛其心。實其腹。弱其志。强其骨。

治，理也。虛其心，無爲也。實其腹，黃帝所謂：聖人服天氣而通神明，亦卽二十章所謂：貴食於母。母，萬物之母，天地之生氣，卽老子之道也。弱其志，志藏乎脾。强其骨，骨屬於腎。脾爲後天之本，腎爲先天之命，且腎爲作强之官，志如過强，不獨虧損其本元，且亦傷其命根。骨何能致强？養其精，塡其髓，此岐伯所謂：骨髓堅固，乃立命之本耳。若謂聖人之治，乃爲腹懷

Chapter 4

四章

道冲而用之或不盈。淵兮似萬物之宗。挫其銳。解其紛。和其光。同其塵。湛兮似或存。吾不知誰之子。象帝之先。

道用冲和，故虛而不盈。四十五章有：大盈若冲，其用不窮。體則淵兮似萬物之所宗，挫銳解紛，乃歸無爲抱一，和光同塵，湛兮神之猶存，誰之子，象帝之先。參看廿五章：有物混成，先天地生。又曰：吾不知其名，字之曰道，强名之曰大。

四 章 Chapter 4

**The Tao is empty, yet when applied is never filled up.
So deep it is, Ah! it seems to be the ancestor of all things.
Blunting sharp edges, resolving confusions,
Diffusing glare, uniting the world:
Such depth, Ah! something seems to exist there.
I do not know whose child it is.
It seems to have existed before the Ancestor.**

In application, Tao blends in, therefore empty and yet never filled. Chapter 45 says, "the greatest fullness seems empty, yet its applications are never exhausted." Thus the "body" of Tao is "so deep, Ah! it seems to be the ancestor of all things", blunting edges and solving quandaries as if all were returned to the Oneness of Non-action. Glare is mitigated and the world united as deeply as if a great spirit were there. Whose child is it? "It seems to have existed before the Ancestor," referring to Chapter 25, "there is a chaotic thing, born before heaven and earth . . . I do not know its name. I reluctantly style it 'Tao', and if forced to, reluctantly describe it 'great'."

五 章 Chapter 5

Heaven and earth are not humane,
treating the myriad things as straw dogs.
The Sage is not humane,
treating the people as straw dogs.

Lecture: The Tao of heaven and earth cannot be called humane. The lives of the myriad things all proceed according to nature. Their passing is no different than that of straw dogs. In ancient times, dogs fashioned from straw were used during ritual sacrifices as substitutes for the real animal. Once they had fulfilled their function, they were cast aside, thus giving rise to the observation of the text that there are no feelings of humanism involved. The Sage's actions are in accord with those of heaven and earth, not showing any favoritism toward mankind through humanism. He treats the people just as heaven and earth treat the myriad things: as if they were straw dogs.

Note: Neither heaven and earth nor the Sage in any way treat humanism as desirable, and it is precisely here that Lao-tzu speaks of humanism as neither beautiful nor good. To say, as Wang Pi does, "Earth produces straw not for the sake of feeding animals, yet animals eat it; produces dogs not for the sake of feeding man, yet men eat them," can be called a glib argument. But do all animals eat straw exclusively, or do men specialize in eating dogs? Wang Pi takes it so in his explanation of Lao-tzu, but is not that vastly oversimplifying the case?

The space between heaven and earth is like a bellows,
empty and yet inexhaustible;
Move it and even more comes out.
Too many words quickly exhaust;
It is not as good as holding to the center.

The bellows referred to is a double-acting piston bellows employed in forging metal. Here it is used figuratively to describe the space between heaven and earth. It is empty, yet never completely exhausted. The more one operates it, the more it produces air, responding ad infinitum. If man would hold to the center, following the example of heaven and earth, he would never again say too much. Too many words speedily lead to exhaustion. Chuang-tzu said: "To maintain the center of the circle is to respond inexhaustibly." That is similar in meaning to this chapter.

Chapter 5

言數窮。不如守中。

屈，竭也。數，音朔，急疾也。橐受籥如櫝，籥鼓橐以管。橐籥者，治工之工具也。以此形容天地，猶鼓風鑪也。以其中虛，故不致竭。動而愈出，以應無窮。人如能守中法天地，則不在多言；多言，必致速窮。莊子所謂：得其環中，以應無窮。亦猶是也。

五章

天地不仁。以萬物爲芻狗。聖人不仁。以百姓爲芻狗。

天地之道，不以仁稱；萬物之生，一任自然。其滅也。與芻狗無異。芻草之爲狗，乃古之尸祝者，祭祀用之，既事，則棄之，言其無涉於仁也。聖人與天地合其德，亦不私與人以仁也。其於百姓亦猶天地之於萬物，與爲芻狗等耳。

按：天地與聖人皆未然以仁爲仁，據此乃直接反對稱仁爲美爲善之說。若謂地不爲獸生芻，而獸食芻；不爲人生狗，而人食狗，可謂佞矣。且獸非盡食芻者，人寧專食狗乎？弼以是而釋老子，何乃太易乎？

天地之間。其猶橐籥乎。虛而不屈。動而愈出。多

Chapter 6

六章

谷神不死。是謂玄牝。玄牝之門。是謂天地根。緜緜若存。用之不勤。

谷神者，卽谷之有神，曰玄牝。神何用稱不死，卽以喩長生久視之道，且玄爲天，牝爲地。天之氣通乎鼻，故玄又爲鼻；地之氣通乎口，牝又爲口。亦以喩人之有口鼻，猶天地之有根也。總此皆稱服氣養氣之用，在乎緜緜若存，用之不勤已耳。此爲老子微妙之門道，未可忽視者也。且喩玄牝謂若谷之虛，虛而不虛，卽謂氣耳。

六章 Chapter 6

The spirit of the valley does not die, and is called Mysterious Female.
The door of the Mysterious Female is called the root of heaven and earth.
It lingers in wisps;
Use it without haste.

Lecture: Valleys have a spirit called Mysterious Female. Why say the spirit does not die? This indicates that it, like Tao, is everlasting and self-perpetuating. According to the *Book of Change,* " 'Mysterious' refers to heaven; 'Female' refers to earth." The breath *(ch'i)* of heaven passes through the nose, hence Mysterious also refers to the nose. The breath *(ch'i)* of the earth passes through the mouth, and Female also refers to the mouth. The nose and mouth of humans may be likened to the root of heaven and earth. In general, all of this has to do with the application of breathing techniques and the cultivation of breath *(ch'i)*, as in "it lingers in wisps; use it without haste." This is the gateway to the traces and marvels of Lao-tzu's Tao, and must not be disregarded. Mysterious Female can be likened to the vacuity of a valley, empty yet not empty, which is to speak of *ch'i*.

Chapter 7

七章

天長地久。天地所以能長且久者。以其不自生。故能長生。是以聖人後其身而身先。外其身而身存。非以其無私邪。故能成其私。

不自生者，故能長生。是有以異乎萬物，以其有生，乃有滅。聖人後其身外其身者，爲無爲也。爲者敗之；爲無爲者，故能成其私。

七章 Chapter 7

Heaven is long lasting and earth is enduring.
The reason why heaven and earth can live long and endure is that they do not live only for themselves.
Therefore, they can produce perpetually.
This is why the Sage puts himself behind yet ends up ahead,
Considers himself an outsider yet finds himself in the mainstream.
Is it not because he is selfless that his Self can be realized?

Lecture: Because heaven and earth do not live for themselves, they can produce perpetually. They differ from the myriad things in that things which are born must die. The Sage puts himself behind and reckons himself an outsider, thus employing Non-action. Those who consciously act, fail; those who enjoy Non-action are able to realize their selves.

Chapter 8

八章

上善若水。水善利萬物。而不爭。處衆人之所惡。故幾於道。

下流，人之所惡，水注之，而不避其卑汚，且善利萬物。謂善者能若水，可稱上善，則近道矣。

居善地。心善淵。與善人。言善信。正善治。事善能。動善時。夫唯不爭。故無尤。

言人能善此七者，如水之無爭，則無尤矣。

八 章 Chapter 8

The best attitude is like water.
Water is a positive benefit to all things without competing with them.
It seeks out those places abominated by man.
Thereby, it approaches the Tao.

Lecture: Low places loathed by people are capital places for water, which does not avoid sewers or cesspools, and yet which benefits everything. If good people can emulate water, they will be in the best position to approach the Tao.

For one's dwelling, choose ground well.
In cultivating one's mind/heart, search the deeps well.
In dealing with people, treat them well.
In speaking, know how to keep one's word.
In governing, rectify the self well.
In serving, do one's best.
In acting, chose the time well.
Only by not competing can one be without reproach.

If a person can do these seven things well, and, like water, avoid competition, he will be free from blame.

Chapter 9

九章

持而盈之。不如其已。揣而梲之。不可長保。

揣，音椳，上聲，度量也。梲，音拙，梁上短柱也，又名侏儒柱。持而盈之，有限耳，不如其止也；雖云度量而梲之，然以其器材弱小，不可長保。

王弼以梲作銳解，似嫌不倫。梲從木，不可作金類解。

金玉滿堂。莫之能守。富貴而驕。自遺其咎。功遂身退。天之道。

不能守則已矣，驕則遺其咎。誰能效天道如春花秋實，功遂而退？

九章 Chapter 9

To grasp after until full is not as good as stopping.
Measure and fit a crossbrace;
It cannot last long.

Lecture: To grasp after until one's hand is full means one has reached the limit; this is not as good as knowing when to stop. Although one measures a crossbrace to fit, it cannot last long since the piece is small and the material weak.

Wang Pi took "crossbrace" to mean "sharp." This is unreasonable. The character for crossbrace belongs to the wood radical and thus cannot have anything to do with metal.

If one's hall is filled with gold and jade,
it cannot be safeguarded.
If one is wealthy and honored,
pride follows,
and one gifts oneself with the faults thereof.
When the work is done, retire;
This is the Tao of heaven.

If something cannot be safeguarded, then let it go; one who is proud will bring trouble upon himself. Who is capable of imitating the Tao of heaven? Who can bring flowers in the Spring and fruit in the Fall, and having done so, retire?

十章 Chapter 10

Can one unify the spirit-of-the-blood and the spirit-of-the-breath
and keep them from separating?

Lecture: The spirits of the blood and breath are referred to in the *Yellow Emperor's Classic on Internal Medicine* and the *Kuan-yin Tzu.* In the latter it says that the nature of blood is to descend and the nature of breath *(ch'i)* to ascend, but when one dies this order is reversed: the spirit of the blood rises and the spirit of the breath descends. The ancients all discussed spirit-of-the-blood and spirit-of-the-breath in this fashion. The text asks whether man can unify these two "spirits" even to the point of avoiding death.

In concentrating the *ch'i* to attain resiliency,
can one be like a baby?

"Concentrating the *ch'i*" refers to breathing, which has been explained earlier. Regarding "to attain resiliency", Ch'i-po said, "let the circulatory systems of blood and *ch'i* flow freely." This is the basis of Lao-tzu's emphasis on the cultivation of *ch'i,* as in the sayings, "the tendons are resilient and the grip is firm", and "reverse old age and become like a child."

In cleansing the Mysterious Vision
can one do it flawlessly?
In loving the people and governing the nation,
can one cause the people to be without knowledge?
In opening and closing heaven's gate,
can one do it without the Female?
In spreading enlightenment in all four directions,
can one do it without conscious action?

"Cleansing the Mysterious Vision" refers to Chapter 1 where it says, "if always without desire, one can observe indescribable marvels; if always desirous, one sees merest traces." If it is granted that man can wash his vision, can it be done cleanly and without blemish? In loving the people and governing the nation, can one cause the people to be without cleverness and without desire? "Female" refers to the trigram *k'un,* "earth", and also means "to close". This is a reference to the *Book of Change.* The "earth" trigram looks like this:☷. The gate of heaven cannot always be open and never close. "Spreading enlightenment far in all four directions" means to hear what is commonly heard and to see what is commonly seen. Can one accomplish this without conscious action? In view of the six questions raised above, what man can harmonize with the Tao? Lao-tzu emphasizes the feminine as in, "know the masculine, yet cleave to the feminine."

Produce and provide a good environment;
Produce but do not possess.
Act but do not control.
Raise but do not harvest.
This is called Profound Teh.

If things are done according to nature, it will not be necessary to act consciously or to insist that others rely on you. "Profound Teh" is that of the earth itself. Compare this with Chapter 65: "Profound Teh is so deep, so far-reaching, it causes things to return and eventually reach Great Confluence." This is what is meant by Tao.

Chapter 10

開闔。能無雌乎。明白四達。能無爲乎。

覽，觀也。疵，病也。常有欲，常無欲，得能觀徼妙者，玄覽也。人縱能滌除其眸子，能淨而無疵乎？愛民治國，能使其無知無欲乎？雌者，坤也，闔也，天門不能長開而無闔也。明白四達者，明四目，達四聰，能無爲乎？以上六問，人誰能合於道乎？老子重守雌，故曰：知其雄，守其雌。乃承此意也。

生之畜之。生而不有。爲而不恃。長而不宰。是謂玄德。

恃，仗也。宰，河上公註：割也。生任自然，復何有爲有恃。玄德者，乃地之德也，參看六十五章：玄德深矣，遠矣，與物反矣。是之謂道。

十章

載營魄抱一。能無離乎。

營黃帝內經所謂：營衞。營，屬血。衞，屬氣。關尹子曰：魂附乎血，魄附乎氣，血性常降，氣性常升，及其死則反之，魂乃上升，魄則下降。營魄者，古注多作魂魄，其詳如是。此乃設問人，載魂魄抱一，能不死而至於離乎？弼營字作漏解，却指營魄爲人之常居處，不知所云。

專氣致柔。能嬰兒乎。

專氣，服氣也，已詳見上。致柔，歧伯曰：筋脉和同。故老氏謂筋柔握固，乃返老還童之候，此尙氣之根據。

滌除玄覽。能無疵乎。愛民治國。能無知乎。天門

Chapter 11

十一章

三十輻。共一轂。當其無有車之用。挻埴以爲器。當其無有器之用。鑿戶牖以爲室。當其無有室之用。

輻，音福，車輪中木之直指者。轂，音谷，輪之中正爲轂，空其中，軸所貫也。輻湊於外，輻數爲三十，轂數爲一，見禮記考工記。挻，和也。埴，粘土也。爲食器也，以及乎室，皆言其中虛，得以爲用。

故有之以爲利。無之以爲用。

以上言有車、器、室，皆當其無有。無者，却以之爲用；有之，祇足爲利耳。下章已解之曰：聖人爲腹不爲目。實其腹者，氣也；盈其谷者，亦氣也。可見腹必如谷之虛，谷却自有腹之實。能是，可得其利，可得其用焉。目務外則傷神，如能存神養氣，若無目，反得其用也。

十一章 Chapter 11

Thirty spokes converge at a single hub:
It is the vacancy that begets the vehicle's usefulness.
Mix clay to make a vessel:
It is the vacancy that makes the vessel useful.
Cut out doors and windows to make a room:
It is the vacancy that constitutes the usefulness of the room.

Lecture: The empty center of the hub is where the axletree fits. Clay vessels are food containers. A room is mentioned. In each case it is the emptiness at the center that is useful.

Therefore, that which is there is an advantage,
But its vacancy is what is useful.

In the above paragraph it says that a vehicle, a vessel, or a room all depend upon their vacancies. The usefulness is just that which is not there; that which is there is a mere advantage. According to the following chapter, the Sage concerns himself with the abdomen and not the eyes. "Reinforcing the abdomen" means *ch'i*; "fill the valley" also means *ch'i*. Hence the abdomen ought to be as empty as the valley, just as the valley is as full (reinforced) as the abdomen. If one can realize this, he can get both advantage and usefulness. If the eyes aggressively look outward, the spirit will suffer harm. If one can allow the spirit to exist unobtrusively and cultivate his breath *(ch'i)* as if he had no eyes, one can also add 'usefulness' to the 'advantage' of the eyes.

Chapter 12

十二章

五色令人目盲。五音令人耳聾。五味令人口爽。馳騁畋獵。令人心發狂。

此皆證明有器爲用之害，終之，則猶爽然若失也。

難得之貨。令人行妨。是以聖人爲腹不爲目。故去彼取此。

不貴難得之貨，故去彼取此。彼者，實則虛之；此者，虛則實之。猶腹之應實，反服氣以虛之；谷之應虛，却以氣而盈之。如目應以視爲用，却使其無用而反視。此老子所謂聖人之道也。若以弼謂腹懷食，則取此，而可以抉去其目矣，又何云：有之以爲利，無之以爲用也？

十二章 Chapter 12

The five colors cause man's eyes to be blinded.
The five tones cause man's ears to be deafened.
The five flavors cause man's palate to be cloyed.
Racing about on horseback and hunting cause man's mind to be maddened.

Lecture: All of the foregoing gives evidence that harm can be done by use of certain 'vessels' (senses). In the extreme, the result is the same as if one had lost his wits.

Hard to obtain merchandise causes mankind to do wrong,
So the Sage concerns himself with the abdomen and not the eyes.
Therefore, he rejects the one and chooses the other.

Do not prize merchandise difficult to obtain: therefore, reject the one and choose the other. The one seems substantial but in fact is hollow; the other seems hollow but in fact is real. This is the same as saying that the abdomen seemingly ought to be filled with substance, but on the contrary one should fill it with breath *(ch'i)*; the valley seems to be empty, but in fact it is filled with vapor *(ch'i)*. By the same token the eyes seemingly ought to be used for looking, but one should use them only to see inwardly. This is what Lao-tzu calls the Tao of the Sage. Wang Pi's interpretation says that one's belly is only for filling with food; that is also to say that one ought to pluck out one's eyes (the Sage is for the belly, not the eyes). If that were so, why does Lao-tzu say "that which is there is an advantage; but its vacancy is what is useful?"

Chapter 13

十三章

寵辱若驚。貴大患若身。何謂寵辱若驚。寵爲下。得之若驚。失之若驚。是謂寵辱若驚。何謂貴大患若身。吾所以有大患者。爲吾有身。及吾無身。吾有何患。

視爾身能否若爾腹，寵得之貴者，猶否若五色、五音、五味乎。若以身爲有身者，終當爲色、音、味所傷，是爲大患。苟視爾身若腹之虛，其如而後盈之以氣，能若是，則可收有爲利，無爲用，又有何患？此之謂外其身，而身存。

故貴以身爲天下。若可寄天下。愛以身爲天下。若可託天下。

貴以身，愛以身，若爲天下，則可寄可託以天下於爾身焉。

十三章 Chapter 13

Favor and disgrace are both alarming.
Treat great calamities as if they were happening to yourself.
What does "favor and disgrace are both alarming" mean?
When favor is conferred upon a lowly position,
it is like a shock.
And when it is taken away, it is like a shock.
This is what is spoken of as
"Favor and disgrace are both alarming."
What does this mean:
"Treat calamities as if they were happening to yourself"?
I am able to feel great calamities because I have a self.
If I have no self, what calamity is there?

Everything depends on whether one can regard himself as he would his abdomen. Is not the effect of favor conferred from those above like the effect of the five colors, the five tones, and the five flavors? If one takes himself too seriously in the end one will suffer from harm inflicted by colors, tones, and flavors, and this is greatly to be avoided. On the other hand, if one can regard himself as being as empty as his abdomen—which later becomes filled with *ch'i*—then one can receive the "advantage of what is there, and the utility of its vacancy." In that case, what calamity could there be? In other words, "(he) considers himself an outsider yet finds himself in the mainstream" (See Chapter 7).

Therefore, only one who values himself as he values the world
is fit to be entrusted with the world.
Only one who loves the world as he loves himself
is worthy of being the trustee of the world.

If one prizes and cherishes himself even as he does the world, then he is fit and worthy to be equally trustee of the world and his self.

十四章 Chapter 14

To look but not see is called *yi*;
To listen but not hear is called *hsi*;
To grasp after but not catch is called *wei*.
These three qualities cannot be understood no matter how much you ask about them,
Yet when intermingled, they form a unity.

Lecture: *Yi* is "to level, to eliminate", as if one were looking at a mountain but seeing a plain. *Hsi* means "small". *Wei* means "obscure, wonderful". "To ask" is "to inquire". What does "these three qualities cannot be understood no matter how much you ask about them" mean? As Chapter 41 says, "a great sound comes from a small noise. A great form has no shape. Tao is hidden and nameless. . . ." thus, unfathomable. "Yet when intermingled, they form a unity," the unity of the Tao. Therefore, the Sage makes this unity his touchstone or structure for understanding the world.

Its upper surface is not bright, its underside is not dark.
In endless procession the unnameable moves on, until it returns to nothingness.
It is the formless form, the image of nothingness.
It may be called *huang-hu*.
Confront it, and you cannot see its face;
Follow it and you cannot see its back.
Hold to the ancient Tao to regulate present realities.
One who is able to comprehend the ancient beginnings may be termed a part of the system of Tao.

"not bright . . . not dark" is to say "yet when intermingled, they form a unity." Formless and imageless, whether one wants to confront it or follow it, it always remains unclear. See Chapter 21, where it says, "Evanescent and elusive it is, yet there is form contained within it. Yes, elusive and evancescent, yet there is substance to it." Again, "Hold to the ancient Tao to regulate present realities." To comprehend this unity is "a part of the system of Tao." All these phrases refer to, "yet when intermingled, they form a unity."

Chapter 14

不皦不昧，謂混一也。繩繩相繼不盡貌。無狀無象，雖欲迎隨而恍惚。參翫廿一章有謂：惚兮恍兮，其中有象，恍兮惚兮，其中有物。又謂：執古之道，以御今之有，知古之一，爲道之紀。皆混一之意耳。

十四章

視之不見名曰夷。聽之不聞名曰希。搏之不得名曰微。此三者不可致詰。故混而爲一。

夷，芟也。雖覩丘陵，等乎平地。希，罕也，少也。微，幽也，妙也。詰，問也。三者不可致詰，何也？四十一章有謂：大音希聲，大象無形，道隱無名。故不可致詰。混而爲一者，道也，故聖人抱一爲天下式。

其上不皦。其下不昧。繩繩不可名。復歸於無物。是爲無狀之狀。無物之象。是謂恍惚。迎之不見首。隨之不見後。執古之道。以御今之有。能知古始。是謂道紀。

十五章 Chapter 15

In ancient times, well educated people were mysterious and in communication with heaven.
Their depth was unfathomable.
Precisely because they were unfathomable they appeared reluctant, even hesitant, like one wading a stream in winter;

Lecture: The system of the Tao can be likened to the decimal system which begins with one and ends at ten. It alternates by tens, therefore it is called a "system."* Those who attained the Tao were in communication with heaven, their profundity unfathomable, and so their manner was one of reluctance: like a person who must cross a stream in winter yet is fearful he will not make it. When face to face with it, every onlooker feels reluctant about the Tao and expresses reluctance over following it. That is why "none can carry it out."

Wary, as if there were dangers on all four sides;
Majestic in appearance;
Yielding, like ice on the verge of melting;
Pure in nature, like uncut jade;
Broad, like a valley;
Mixed, as if muddy.

This describes how profound the Tao is, and how unfathomable.

Who can still muddy water and gradually make it clear?
Who can make the still gradually become alive through activity?
Those who maintain the Tao do not want to be full.
Just because they are not full
they can avoid wearing out and being replaced.

Lao-tzu comments, "exhaust, and become renewed," therefore, avoid old age and replacement is not necessary. See Chapter 22. Who knows that muddy water, when stilled, becomes clear; that living beings, if they seek tranquility, will extend their lifetimes? The Tao does not desire to be full, and therefore avoids the conditions necessary for replacement. As it says in Chapter 80, "cause people to revert to using knotted ropes." Chapter 39 says, "all things attained Oneness and became alive." Therefore I believe the second sentence of the text above must be mistaken and ought to read "calm the active and gradually become alive." That is, through tranquility attain peaceful Oneness until gradually becoming alive.

* *Translator's Note:* These words indicate a continuation of the discussion of "system" which was the subject of the previous chapter.

Chapter 15

者不欲盈。夫唯不盈。故能蔽不新成。

老主敝則新，故蔽之，不使新成，見二十二章。誰知水濁，止而靜以徐清。物動，安以久之徐生。道不欲盈，故蔽掩之，不使其有所新成，猶八十章所謂：使復結繩而用之。又三十九章謂：萬物得一以生。故吾以第二句必有訛誤，應作：動以安之徐生。安之，然後可得寧一，以致徐生也。

十五章

古之善爲士者。微妙玄通。深不可識。夫唯不可識。故强爲之容。豫焉，若冬涉川。

紀，綱紀也。數起於一，終於十，十則更，故曰紀。得道者，微妙玄通，以其深不可識也，故强爲之形容，若冬涉川，望之者，莫不猶豫焉，有難色，是以莫能行也。

猶兮若畏四鄰。儼兮其若容。渙兮若冰之將釋。敦兮其若樸。曠兮其若谷。混兮其若濁。

猶若畏四鄰，儼若有容，渙若冰釋，敦若樸，曠若谷，混若濁，亦形容道之深，不可識已耳。

孰能濁以靜之徐清。孰能安以久動之徐生。保此道

Chapter 16

十六章

致虛極。守靜篤。萬物並作。吾以觀復。夫物芸芸。各復歸其根。歸根曰靜。是謂復命。復命曰常。知常曰明。不知常。妄作凶。

虛極靜篤，萬物並作，爲無爲也。至芸芸生意極繁，終各歸根，而復其靜之常。復，陽復也。不知常者，眞昧妄作，未有不殆。

知常容。容乃公。公乃王。王乃天。天乃道。道乃久。沒身不殆。

容無所不包，公無所不平，王無所不往而歸之。天，大也。天法道，道尤大，而且玄，久則無極，體道者能是，則不復有沒身之殆哉！

十六章 Chapter 16

Attain utmost emptiness.
Maintain profound tranquility.
All things are stirring about.
I watch their cycle.
Things flourish, and each returns to its root.
Returning to the root is called tranquility;
This is what is meant by returning to one's basic nature.
Returning to one's basic nature is called constancy.
To understand constancy is called enlightening.
Not to understand constancy is blindly to do unfortunate things.

Lecture: Utmost emptiness, profound tranquility, all things stir about—this is the enactment of Non-action. Things flourish yet in the end each returns to its root, returns to the constancy of its tranquility. "Cycle" is a "return to *yang*," a phenomenon associated with the *yang* or active principle.* Those who do not understand constancy are blind to the truth and blunder into doing wrong. Disaster will surely follow.

Understanding constancy, one gains a capacity for forbearance.
If forbearing, one can be just.
If just, one can administer the affairs of state morally.
If one can administer the affairs of state morally,
then he can communicate with heaven.
To communicate with heaven is to be in accord with the Tao.
If in accord with the Tao, one is everlasting,
And even though his body ceases to be, he is not destroyed.

"Forbearance" includes the capacity to be all-encompassing. "Just" means to be fair to all. To "administer the affairs of state morally" means everyone turns to the administrator for leadership. To "communicate with heaven" is to be in communication with all people. Heaven patterns itself after the Tao. The Tao is all-encompassing, profound, everlasting, and so without limits. One who embodies the Tao is never again in danger of losing his self.

* *Translator's Note:* "Tranquility" is associated with the *yin* or passive principle. When the *yin* reaches its ultimate it changes to *yang* in accordance with the cycle of polarity, just as the first moment after noon is night. A.M. changes to P.M.

Chapter 17

十七章

太上下。知有之。其次親而譽之。其次畏之。其次侮之。信不足焉。有不信焉。

太上下，卽太古之天下也，有知之。次者親近而稱譽之。又其次者畏之，若冬涉川焉。又其次者，直侮之，不獨大笑而已。有信不足者，且有不信者矣。

悠兮其貴言。功成事遂。百姓皆謂我自然。

若言悠兮其貴者，成事，人以爲自然，却不知爲無爲者，道法自然耳。

十七章 Chapter 17

From times immemorial there have been some who have known (Tao).
There have also been those who were sympathetic toward it and praised it.
There have been those who have feared it.
There have been those who have ridiculed it.
There have been those who were not true enough to it,
And so there have been those who have not been true to it at all.

Lecture: T'ai-shang-hsia means that in the time of great antiquity *(t'ai-ku-chih t'ien-hsia)* there have been those who knew it (the Tao).* There have been those who have feared the Tao as they would fear "crossing a stream in mid-winter." Moreover, there have been those who have gone beyond merely laughing at it, who have confronted it with ridicule.

How invaluable are the words,
"When an accomplishment is achieved and the task finished,
People say it was only natural."

What the people should appreciate is that the task is finished, but the people consider it as only natural. They do not know that this is the result of Non-action and that Tao works according to nature.

* *Translator's Note:* This interpretation accords with that of Ho-shang Kung and not with that of Wang Pi.

十八章 Chapter 18

If the great Tao is lost,
Humanism and justice appear.
When intelligence and cleverness arise,
So does gross hypocrisy.

Lecture: The great Tao is described in Chapter 25 as "the Mother of all under heaven." When the Mother was alive, everything in the world was her child. "If the great Tao is lost" all things become helpless, motherless children. When we see those who love orphans we call them humane; those who give to orphans are just. When intelligence and cleverness arise in men, like motherless children they plot to increase individual enrichment and gross hypocrisy develops. This is the basic reason why Lao-tzu opposes humanism and justice.

Note: Lao-tzu says that after the great Tao is lost, humanism and justice appear. But since the great Tao has no substance, no origin, and no name, how can it be lost? If, between heaven and earth, there were no humans, then even though the great Tao were not lost, what would it matter whether it existed? If mankind were to disregard humanism and justice, it would be equivalent to heaven without the qualities of *yin* and *yang,* earth without the qualities of hardness and softness, and a return to primal chaos.* If this were the case, then why bother to return to the age of knot-tying? Tying knots is also "intelligence and cleverness." If one were to speak strictly in terms of non-action, even tying knots would be too active. As for the gross hypocrisy of mankind, it is as if heaven and earth had only the qualities of *yin* and softness. When the qualities of *yang* and hardness lose the affirmative, then the qualities of *yin* and softness predominate. When humanism and justice are not sharp and clear, then gross hypocrisy arises. Yet Lao-tzu himself praises the use of orthodoxy (i.e. uprightness) to administer government, so even if gross hypocrisy exists there should be no great worry.

**When the six relationships fall into discord,
Filial piety and parental affection arise.
When a nation falls into darkness and confusion,
Patriotic ministers arise.**

The "six relationships falling into discord" means that neither parents, children, elder brothers, younger brothers, husbands, nor wives act according to their positions. If this were the case, a minimal knowledge of the relations between parents and children would easily pass for filial piety and parental affection. If everyone behaved properly, whether as affectionate parents or as filial children, would filial piety and parental affection need names? If nations were all as well-governed as during the golden age of the T'ang and Yu Dynasties, then would such titles as patriotic ministers be necessary?

Note: Lao-tzu is speaking from the reverse side of things, and he has his reasons, but I wonder what brought the six relationships into existence? How did they fall out of harmony? How could there have been a "golden age" of government; how did this "golden age" fall into darkness and confusion? To answer that everything was a product of Non-action would be overdoing it. Lao-tzu alone desires to live according to Non-action, while those who practice plain Action outnumber him a billion to one. From this it is possible to deduce that what Lao-tzu advocates cannot be carried out.

* *Translator's Note:* Traditionally, *yang* and *yin* refer to the basic qualities of heaven, hardness and softness are the qualities of earth, and male and female are the qualities of mankind. Heaven, earth, and mankind form a trinity of "three powers" (or agents) *(san-ts'ai)* which comprise the metaphysical cosmos of traditional Chinese thought.

Chapter 18

六親不和有孝慈。國家昏亂有忠臣。

六親不和者，父不父，子不子，兄不兄，弟不弟，夫不夫，妻不妻，及是時也，稍有能知父子之道者，便以爲孝慈矣。倘天下皆能父父子子者，又何有孝慈之稱也？國家倘皆如唐虞郅治，又何有忠臣之稱哉？

按：老氏從反面說來，亦自有其理。請問何以爲六親？何以爲不和？何以爲郅治，何以爲昏亂？若悉稱無爲者，此說已成餘贅矣。然欲爲無爲者，老氏一人而已。爲有爲者，豈止億萬萬兆人而已哉？此老氏之說，其莫之能行也，可知矣。

十八章

大道廢。有仁義。慧智出。有大僞。

大道者，乃廿五章所謂：天下母也，母在，皆孩視天下也。大道廢，則猶有無母何恃之子焉，見愛之者，謂之仁；與之者，謂之義耳。慧智出者，亦猶無母失恃之子，各謀自立以生存，大僞亦從而生焉。此老子反仁義之原則。

按：老氏謂大道廢，然後有仁義。大道原無物，本無始，亦無名，孰能廢之。若天地中無人，則大道不廢，又安得而存焉？人如舍仁義，則猶天之無陰陽，地之無剛柔，歸混沌矣，何勞反結繩而用之？且結繩，亦慧智也。若以無爲而言，結繩猶多事矣。然人之有大僞，亦猶天地之有陰柔。陽剛不振，而後陰柔著；仁義不明，而後大僞興。老聃自詡以正爲治者，縱有大僞，又何患哉！

Chapter 19

十九章

絕聖棄智。民利百倍。絕仁棄義。民復孝慈。絕巧棄利。盜賊無有。此三者以爲文不足。故令有所屬。見素抱樸。少私寡欲。

所謂絕聖仁巧，棄智義利，則利百倍，可復孝慈，而盜賊無有者，其意以爲聖可聖乃有爲也，六十五章所謂古之善爲道者，非以明民，將以愚之。三十八章所謂：失道而後德，失德而後仁，失仁而後義。四十九章所謂：天下渾其心，聖人皆孩之。此乃老子之所謂聖人也。且絕聖仁巧，此三者乃老子一人之言，由來無此明文，故謂文不足。

按：猶龍氏，文思嶄新，邁無前古。然此章既稱見素抱樸，少私寡欲，又安用民利百倍？既絕人道之仁義，又何希孝慈之可復？人眩玄談，而吾却以爲贅矣。

十九章 Chapter 19

Divorce wisdom and abandon intelligence,
And the people will benefit a hundred-fold.
Divorce humanism and abandon justice,
And the people will return to filial piety and parental affection.
Divorce shrewdness and abandon selfishness,
And there will be no thieves.
I believe these three statements show that words are inadequate.
The people should be made to adhere to these principles:
"Look to the origins and maintain purity;
Diminish self and curb desires."

Lecture: What is described as "divorce wisdom . . . humanism . . . shrewdness; abandon intelligence . . . justice . . . selfishness . . . and thereby benefit a hundred-fold . . . return to filial piety and parental affection . . . and there will be no thieves" all points to the idea that a sage who can put his wisdom to work is Acting. Lao-tzu wants to keep the people ignorant (Chapter 65): "The ancients who were most adept at ruling did not try to enlighten the people, but . . . gradually made them stupid." Chapter 38 says, "If Tao is lost, Teh appears. If Teh is lost, humanism appears. If humanism is lost, justice appears." Chapter 49 says, "(the Sage's) mind merges with the world. The Sage treats everyone as his children." These are all descriptions of Lao-tzu's Sage. Moreover, the three sentences, "divorce wisdom . . . humanism . . . shrewdness" are the words of Lao-tzu alone, and, before him, never found clear expression. Therefore the text says, "words are inadequate."

Note: Dragon-like, Lao-tzu's essays and thoughts were revolutionary, easily surpassing what had gone before. However, he says, "look to the origins and maintain purity; diminish the self and curb desires." That being so, then of what use are the words, "the people will benefit a hundred-fold?" Furthermore, if man discards humanism and justice—which Confucius says are basic tenets of the Tao of Mankind—why hope for a return to parental affection and filial piety? Some indulge in imaginative speculation over such issues, but I feel they are superfluous.

二十章

Chapter 20

Divorce learning and one will lose anxiety.
How much difference is there between yea and nay?
How much distance is there between good and bad?
What others fear, I must fear.

Lecture: Yea and nay indicate a comparison. Chapter 48 says, "In pursuing knowledge, one accumulates daily; in practicing Tao, one loses daily." One deduces from this that by divorcing oneself from learning, not only will he have no anxieties, he ought to undergo the loss of all loss. The distance between good and bad is in Chapter 2, "if everyone understands the beautiful as beauty, it is ugly. If everyone understands goodness as good, it is not good at all." The difference between good and bad is the exact opposite of what we expect. Compare the lines, "what others fear, I must fear" with Chapter 49, where it says, "I am kind to the kind. I am also kind to the unkind." If everyone is treated with equal kindness, then what is there to fear?

Wildly, endlessly, all men are merry,
as though feasting upon beef
or sitting on the veranda in the spring sunshine.
I alone remain uncomitted,
like an infant who has not yet smiled.

"Merry" means the emotions are engaged. "Beef" refers to the sacrificial ox used during imperial ritual. A paraphrase of the above text would be, "it has been going on for such a long time—sigh—and they are still carrying on like this. Man's unbridled enjoyment seems as vast as an ocean—with no shore in sight—yet I still remain as placid as an infant in swaddling clothes."

I alone seem as mindless as one who has no home to return to.
Everyone else has enough and more,
Yet I alone seem to be left with nothing.
What a fool's mind I have!

How muddled I am!
Most people seek brightness and clarity.
I alone seek dullness and darkness.
Most people are imaginative and observant.
I alone am stifled and mum;
I am as unmoved as the ocean,
As ceaseless as the wind high in the sky.
Everyone else has something to do;
I alone am ignorant and dull.
I alone am different from the rest in that I value taking sustenance from the Mother.

"Aimless" means lackadaisical, listless. "Muddled" means to have lost everything. "I alone am ignorant and dull. I alone differ from the rest in that I value taking sustenance from the Mother." "Mother" is the Mother of all things—that is, air or breath *(ch'i)*—and this follows the same thread as the preceding words, "like an infant who has not yet smiled." Thus it is that practicing breathing techniques is likened to sucking milk from the breast.

Note: The words "I alone am different from the rest," and six other sentences in this chapter should be taken together with the words of Chapter 57, where it says, "I practice Non-action . . . I love tranquility . . . I do not interfere in anything . . . I am without desires . . ." This gives us a view of how Lao-tzu stresses ego. One who is egocentric cannot alleviate his notions of intention, necessity, and insistence. This is diametrically opposed to the views of Confucius. Herein lies a crucial difference between Lao-tzu and Confucius.

Chapter 20

儽儽兮若無所歸。衆人皆有餘。而我獨若遺。我愚人之心也哉。沌沌兮。俗人昭昭。我獨昏昏。俗人察察。我獨悶悶。澹兮其若海。飂兮若無止。衆人皆有以。而我獨頑似鄙。我獨異於人。而貴食於母。

儽，音壘，懶懈貌。沌，音屯，渾沌貌。飂，音聊，高風貌。遺，失也。我雖獨頑似鄙，而有以異於人者，而貴食於母。母，萬物之母也，氣也，應上文：如嬰兒之未孩。故謂服天氣，猶代乳食也。

按：此章所謂我獨異於人等六句，與五十七章：我無爲，以及我好靜，我無事，我無欲等句並觀，可見老子之重我見；重我見者對於意必固三字，皆不可缺少，此正與孔子相反，可見老與孔之異同，焦點在此。

二十章

絕學無憂。唯之與阿。相去幾何。善之與惡。相去若何。人之所畏。不可不畏。

與阿之阿，比也。四十八章有：爲學日益，爲道日損。可見絕學非但無憂，猶宜損之又損也。善惡之相去，已見第二章：天下皆知美之爲美，斯惡已，皆知善之爲善，斯不善已。其相去適得其反。人之所畏，不可不畏，與四十九章：不善者吾亦善之。可參閱也。苟善之，則何畏之有？

荒兮其未央哉。衆人熙熙。如享太牢。如春登臺。我獨泊兮其未兆。如嬰兒之未孩。

熙熙，和也。太牢，天子祭用牛。歎荒遠兮其無極，此衆人享樂之無涯涘，我猶泊止在襁褓時也。

二十一章 Chapter 21

The countenance of a person of high moral cultivation comes from living according to the Tao.
The phenomenon of Tao is so elusive and so evanescent.
Evanescent and elusive it is, yet there is a form contained within it.
Yes, elusive and evanescent, yet there is substance to it.
So vacant and so dark, yet there is a vital essence there.
This vital essence is very real.
It is verifiable.
From past to present its name has not been obliterated, because it is evident in the origins of all things.
How do I know the circumstances of the origins of all things?
Exactly by this phenomenon.

Lecture: The countenance of a person of high moral cultivation can only come directly from cleaving to the Tao. The Tao becomes Tao when in the midst of evanescence and elusiveness there is form and substance; when in the midst of vacancy and darkness there is an essence which is very real. Tao is verifiable, since throughout time its name has never been lost. The origins of all living creatures are evident in it, and by extension, one can know the circumstances of the phenomenon of the Tao. This Tao, although elusive, evanescent, vacant, and dark, by dint of the form and substance within it reveals the presence of an essence so real it is a verification of Tao which indicates how high one's moral cultivation is. In the eighty-one chapters of the *Tao Teh Ching*, there are a total of seventeen properties ascribed to *Teh* (sometimes rendered as "moral cultivation," as in the text of this chapter) including "primal *Teh*," "best *Teh*," and "everlasting *Teh*," to name a few. The more mysterious the Tao is, the more real *Teh* is; the more vacant Tao is, the more concrete *Teh* is; the more obscure Tao is, the more obvious *Teh* is. When Tao is cultivated in a person, his *Teh* is "real;" when cultivated in a family, its *Teh* has "more influence;" when cultivated in a village, state, or in the world, then *Teh* is "lasting," "abundant," or "universal." This theme is carried to the point that when Lao-tzu's Sage holds the left half of a tally-stick in comparison, those with *Teh* keep their half, while those without *Teh* forfeit theirs. This is the reason why the word *k'ung*, translated as "high" in "high moral development," is vital to the text and may not be explained away as an "empty" (meaningless) word. Tao takes *Teh* as its root and trunk. If this root is made "hollow" or "empty," the Tao has no base on which to stand. If one does not allow this single word its true meaning, then the five-thousand word *Tao Teh Ching* will be shaken to its foundations.

Note: This chapter describes what it is about the Tao that makes it the Tao. Those who sincerely desire to approach the Tao of Lao-tzu will have no place to get a hand-hold without this chapter and Chapter 14. Lao-tzu has his own Tao, attained through breathing techniques *(fu ch'i chih chiao)*. If those who wish to cultivate their health and enrich their lives follow the principles of Non-action and No-desire and practice them seriously and with discipline, they will certainly get results. That is why the text says the Tao has form, substance, and essence so real that it is verifiable. How do I know that Lao-tzu is capable of all this? When I was young I was sick unto death, and to make a long story short, I followed Lao-tzu's method of cultivating *ch'i* (psycho-physiological energy consisting of an amalgram of breath, blood, and mind), enabling me to lengthen my life more than forty years. How can I ever forget the rewards Lao-tzu has given me? Nevertheless, I am a human being and as such must speak of the Tao of Mankind. My real desire, therefore, is to follow Confucius to the end. If it were otherwise, even though I lived as long as P'eng Chu (reputed to have lived to the age of 800), of what use would my life be to mankind? Although to seek a long life has its purposes, they are at a far remove from the study of the Tao of Mankind.

Chapter 21

言道惟隱，言德愈著。如修之於身，其德乃眞；修之於家，其德乃餘；以及修之於鄉於國於天下，而其德乃長，乃豐，乃普。甚至謂聖人執左劵，有德司契，無德司徹。是故孔德之孔，不可作空字解。道乃以德爲根，如掘空其根，則道失所依據矣。倘認此一字未眞，則五千言之道德經，根本爲之動搖矣。

按：此章乃形容道之所以爲道。必欲究老子之道者，舍此章與前十四章，則無從着手矣。老子自有其道，乃得服氣之效。求養生者，如法其無爲無欲，篤而行之，意者必可獲其信驗。故謂有象有物，有精甚眞有信也。我何以知老子能是？以少日病甚欲絕，略從其養氣之法行之，已得延長四十餘年，此老氏之德於我者，何敢忘也？雖然，我，人也，應言人道，乃所願學孔子，以爲壽縱能齊彭籛，於人類無裨也。然而學長生又一事也，究與人道有一間耳。

二十一章

孔德之容。惟道是從。道之爲物。惟恍惟惚。惚兮恍兮。其中有象。恍兮惚兮。其中有物。窈兮冥兮。其中有精。其精甚眞。其中有信。自古及今。其名不去。以閱衆甫。吾何以知衆甫之狀哉。以此。

孔，甚也。容，貌也。言甚有德之爲容，惟能從於道也。道之爲道，於恍惚中，其有象有物；於窈冥中，其有精，甚眞。可以信驗之者，是以自古及今，其名之不得去也。衆，多也。甫，始也。謂可閱及萬物之始，推而知其狀也以是。夫道，雖云恍惚，且窈冥，惟其中有象有物，有精甚眞，有信者，卽形容甚有其德也。道德經八十一章，讚德者，如元德、上德、常德之類，俱不同，凡十有七見，言道惟玄，言德愈眞；言道惟虛，言德愈實；

二十二章 Chapter 22

Yield, and become whole.
Bend, and become straight.
Hollow out, and become filled.
Exhaust, and become renewed.
Small amounts are obtainable;
Large amounts are confusing.
Therefore the Sage embraces the Oneness of the Tao
And becomes a guide for the whole world.

Lecture: The ancient phrase has it, "yield, and become whole," which means making concessions in order to achieve a greater result in the totality of events. Lao-tzu invokes examples. The sayings "bend . . . straight," "hollow . . . filled," "exhaust . . . renewed," and those which follow later, such as "know the masculine, cleave to the feminine," "know the bright, keep to the dull," "understand glory; keep to humility," or "sick of sickness, you will gain health," all express parallel ideas. The one who can practice the dictum, "small amounts are obtainable; large amounts are confusing . . . take Oneness as a guide," penetrates to the very core and source of the Tao and will not be confused.

He does not focus on himself and so is brilliant.
He does not seek self-justification and so becomes his own evidence.
He does not make claims and hence is given the credit.
He does not compete with anyone, and hence no one in the world can compete with him.
How can that which the ancients expressed as "yield, and become whole" be meaningless?
If wholly sincere, you will return to them.

The meaning of this paragraph is more or less similar to a statement in the *Book of Change,* "the goal of the noble man is to 'be humble in the face of adulation and thus be a shining light; be able to endure the most extreme degradation.' "

Note: When Lao-tzu introduces the quote from the *Classic on Rites*, "yield, and become whole," he means it in a theoretical sense. When Tseng-tzu was on the brink of death he summoned his disciples and said, "Examine my feet, examine my hands. The *Book of Odes* says, 'In fear and trembling as if hanging over an abyss or treading on thin ice.' From now on I know release from committing faults, my little ones!" Tseng-tzu's words* come from his personal experience in life and so are much more meaningful than the theories of Lao-tzu.

* *Translator's Note:* Tseng-tzu (Tseng Shen, 505—c. 436 B.C.) was an outstanding disciple of Confucius and was noted for his filial piety. In this death-bed quote (see *Analects* 8:3), Tseng-tzu is referring to the dictum that a filial child should take care of his body so that when he meets his ancestors in the after-life he will be as whole as when he was born into the world. This is one of the goals of the noble man.

Chapter 22

門弟子曰：啓予足，啓予手，詩云：戰戰兢兢，如臨深淵，如履薄冰。而今以後，吾知免夫，小子。而曾子乃以心身體驗，其趣愈於老氏矣。

二十二章

曲則全。枉則直。窪則盈。敝則新。少則得。多則惑。是以聖人抱一。爲天下式。

窪，音洼，與窊同。古語謂：曲則全，卽委曲求全也。老氏援例，申之以枉直窪盈敝新，與下文，知雄守雌，知白守黑，知榮守辱，及病病不病等語，皆充其意也。少得多惑，抱一爲式者，究本窮源，不致或惑也。

不自見故明。不自是故彰。不自伐故有功。不自矜故長。夫唯不爭。故天下莫能與之爭。古之所謂曲則全。豈虛語。誠全而歸之。

此節大致與易之謙尊而光，卑不可踰，君子之終也，之意近似。

按：老子引禮經，謂全而歸之，乃從理論一面而言。曾子臨終，召

二十三章 Chapter 23

It is nature's way to say little,
For hurricanes do not last a whole morning
nor thunderstorms all day.
What causes them?
Heaven and earth.
If even heaven and earth are unable to persevere for long,
Then how much longer can man?

Lecture: It is in harmony with Tao when speech is short and natural. Chapter 43 says, "few in the world attain wordless teaching and the benefit of Non-action." This is the exact opposite of "too many words quickly exhaust," in Chapter 5. Although caused by heaven and earth, hurricanes and thundershowers cannot last long, because they are too furious and violent and therefore fall outside natural laws for enduring phenomena. Lao-tzu's explanation reflects contempt for human striving.

Therefore, there are those who practice the Tao.
Those who behave according to the Tao are in communication with the Tao.
Those who behave according to Teh are in communication with Teh.
Those who have lost the Tao and Teh are in communication with failure.
Those in communication with Tao are also joyously received by Tao.
Those in communication with Teh are also joyously received by Teh.
Those in communication with failure are also welcomed by failure.
Some are not true enough to the Tao,
And so there are those who are not true to it at all.

Those who are in communication with the Tao are in turn welcomed by the Tao. Because of this communion, the attainment of the Tao is a joy. The same reactions hold for those who are in communication with Teh, etc. The same idea is expressed in the *Book of Change:* "similar tones respond to each other (sympathetic vibration); beings which have similar 'life-force' (*ch'i,* psycho-physiological energy, breath) seek each other." The above text also says, "those in communication with failure are also welcomed by failure," which one must put beside the text of Chapter 38: "Thus, if Tao is lost, Teh appears. If Teh is lost, humanism appears. If humanism is lost, justice appears." With rumination, one will understand Lao-tzu's point: if people fail in practicing Teh, they will be happy to accept humanism. Those who have failed in following Tao, and then Teh, because they do not understand them, thereby accept humanism, or failing that, justice, and are perfectly happy to do so. "Some are not true enough to the Tao, and so there are those who are not true to it at all," means that those who have failed in following either the Tao or Teh lack faith, which finally leads to complete faithlessness.

Chapter 23

同於道者，道亦樂得之，以其道同，故得道爲樂。同於德者亦然。此易所謂同聲相應，同氣相求之意，又謂：同於失者，失亦樂得之，須與三十八章：故失道而後德，失德而後仁，失仁而後義。參閱，方可得其旨趣。謂同爲失道者，而樂得其德也，同爲失德者，而樂得其仁也。然既失道失德者，以其不明道與德，是以得仁與義，亦以爲樂也。信不足焉，有不信焉，此謂失道與德者，有信不足者，乃失道與德或不信者之所致也。

二十三章

希言自然。故飄風不終朝。驟雨不終日。孰爲此者。天地。天地尚不能久。而況於人乎。

希言自然，希，少也。少言出乎自然，則合乎道。四十三章有：不言之教，無爲之益，天下希及之。正與多言數窮相反。故飄風驟雨，雖天地爲之，不能久也，以其過疾與暴，有以失乎自然，此亦有以嫌人爲之無益也。

故從事於道者。道者同於道。德者同於德。失者同於失。同於道者。道亦樂得之。同於德者。德亦樂得之。同於失者。失亦樂得之。信不足焉。有不信焉。

Chapter 24

二十四章

企者不立。跨者不行。自見者不明。自是者不彰。自伐者無功。自矜者不長。其在道也。曰餘食贅行。物或惡之。故有道者不處。

企，音器，舉踵望也。自見自是自伐自矜，與廿二章同出。此節却又解之曰：食之剩餘，行之不當，有道者不處也。

二十四章 Chapter 24

If one is on tiptoe, he cannot stand firm.
If one stands with straddled legs he cannot walk.
One who is fascinated with himself is not clear-sighted.
If one seeks self-justification, he will not be his own evidence.
If one makes claims, he will not get credit.
If one considers his successes important, he will not endure.
According to Tao, these are called "left-over food" and "superfluous behavior," and go against natural law.
Hence, a man of Tao spurns them.

Self-fascination, self-righteousness, self-promotion, and gloating are all products of Chapter 22. Another explanation for this section might be that a man of Tao will not travel the path of eating to excess or doing what is questionable.

二十五章 Chapter 25

There is a chaotic thing, born before heaven and earth,
So silent, so empty, unique and unchanging, circling endlessly.
It could be considered the Mother of all under heaven.
I do not know its name.
I reluctantly style it "Tao,"
And if forced to, reluctantly describe it as "great."

Lecture: "Chaotic thing" means the One, or Tao, that was born even before heaven and earth. "Silent" means peaceful, quiet; "empty" means vacant, "unique" means different from all else, without match. Heaven and earth might, at some time, be destroyed, but the Tao will never vanish; it is said to be changeless. "Circling endlessly" means circulating in all directions: north, east, south, west, up, and down, without end, becoming the mother of all creatures. Tao has no name, so the text says "forced" to describe it.

"Great" can be described as going ever onward.
"Going ever onward" can be described as going far.
"Going far" can be described as returning.
Hence, the Tao is great.
Heaven is great, earth is great, and mankind, also, is great.
There are four phenomena of greatness in the universe,
and mankind is one of them.
Mankind follows the ways of the earth,
The earth follows the ways of heaven,
Heaven follows the ways of Tao,
And Tao follows the ways of Nature.

"Going far" means going limitlessly. "Returning" means completing a circle and returning. Tao is great, equally as great as heaven and earth, and mankind is also great because it is one of the three elements of the universe (heaven, earth, and mankind). Some editions of Lao-tzu make it ". . . the king, also, is great," which brings in Action and slants the meaning. The proper edition has it as "mankind." Why does mankind "follow the ways of the earth?" Because the earth's Teh is fecundity. Why does earth "follow the ways of heaven?" Because *yin* and *yang* interact. Why does heaven "follow the ways of Tao?" Because the Tao melds with it to form unity. And why does Tao "follow the ways of Nature?" It does so, because it is part of Nature.

Chapter 25

，人亦大者，人居三才之一也。或作王亦大者，以其有爲而偏着也。從善本應作人爲是，人何以法地？以其有生畜之德。地何以法天？以其有陰陽之道。天何以法道？以其能混成一也。道何以法自然？以其能從自然而然也。

二十五章

有物混成。先天地生。寂兮寥兮。獨立不改。周行而不殆。可以爲天下母。吾不知其名。强字之曰道。强爲之名曰大。

混成者，一也，道也，乃先天地而生。寂，靜也。寥，虛也。獨立無對也。天地有時或毀，道不滅，故曰不改。周行，猶周流六虛而不盡也，乃爲天下萬物之母。道無名，故曰：强名之耳。

大曰逝。逝曰遠。遠曰反。故道大。天大地大人亦大。域中有四大。而人居其一焉。人法地。地法天。天法道。道法自然。

逝，往也。遠，無極也。反，周而復也。故曰道大，與天地同大

Chapter 26

二十六章

重爲輕根。靜爲躁君。是以聖人終日行。不離輜重。雖有榮觀。燕處超然。奈何萬乘之主。而以身輕天下。輕則失本。躁則失君。

輕，猶枝葉。重，猶本也。躁，猶流火。靜，猶日也。輜重，行李也。猶言聖人雖止終日行，亦不離衣食之具，是亦不離其本也。榮觀，河上公注：謂宮闕也。雖有榮觀，猶未若平居而超然也。萬乘之主，輕則失本，躁則失其分也，誠不可以身輕天下耳。

二十六章 Chapter 26

Heaviness is the root of lightness.
Tranquility is the master of emotion.
That is why the sage,
practicing Tao all day long,
does not part from his baggage.
Although he may have a grand mansion,
still his daily life remains simple.
How can one be lord of a large state
and behave lightly before the world?
If light, his root will be lost;
If emotional, his master will be lost.

Lecture: "Lightness" is comparable to twigs and leaves; "heaviness" may be likened to the roots and trunk, or basis. Emotions are like shooting stars. Tranquility is like sunlight. Baggage means the necessities of life. Even though the Sage is traveling only for a single day, he does not leave his "baggage"—food and clothing—just as he will not abandon his roots. According to Ho-shang Kung, "grand mansion" means a palace. The Sage, although he has a palace to live in, nevertheless leads a life which is in no way out of the ordinary. The lord of a large state might behave lightly, thereby losing his roots, or become emotional and lose his judgment. Truly, one cannot behave lightly before the world.

二十七章 Chapter 27

The best walking leaves no tracks.
The best speech is flawless.
The best calculation needs no counting slips.
The best latch has no bolt, yet cannot be opened.
The best knot uses no rope, yet cannot be untied.

Lecture: In Chapter 8 Lao-tzu has praise for "the best attitude is like water" and then illustrates the principle seven times. In this chapter he mentions five examples: walking, speaking, calculating, latching, and knotting. He is describing the existence of such endless wonders as the "enactment of Non-action" reaching the point of producing "nothing left undone."

That is why the Sage is always good at saving people,
and therefore abandons nobody.
He is always good at saving things
and therefore abandons nothing.
This is called *hsi ming*.

Hsi means "harmonizing with" and "according to." *Hsi-ming* ("harmonizing with (and according to) the attributes of things") is an old saying. In Chapter 81 are the words, "the way of nature benefits and does not harm." The Sage and heaven communicate with the same Teh, as exemplified by Emperor Yü and his system of canals and irrigation; Prince Millet and his sowing of the grains; or King Wen, who cared for the people as if their suffering were his own. Each was "always good at saving people, and therefore abandon(ed) nobody." Their kindness extended even to beasts and insects, so that each was "always good at saving things, and therefore abandon(ed) nothing." Theirs were acts not just according to the attributes of all creatures, but actually conforming with the way of nature.

Therefore good people are examples for mediocre people,
While mediocre people have the potential to be good people.

Not to appreciate the example, not to cherish the potential,
Is to be far astray, regardless of intelligence.
This is an essential tenet of the Tao.

If examples and potentials can not only fulfill their capacities but also be transformed, nothing will be bad. If, however, neither the example is appreciated nor the potential cherished, there will be confusion. Knowledge of this is essential. When Lao-tzu says do away with sagacity and reject wisdom, he is not referring to this sacred knowledge; rather, this knowledge is his name for the sacred wisdom of the Tao.

Chapter 27

已。

故善人者。不善之師。不善人者。善人之資。不貴其師。不愛其資。雖智大迷。是謂要妙。

師之與資，不獨能得其用，且俱與之化焉，無不善也。不貴愛其師之與資，則迷惑矣，知此爲要妙。然此所稱之智，非絕聖棄智之智，乃老聃所稱道之聖智也。

二十七章

善行無轍跡。善言無瑕謫。善數不用籌策。善閉無關楗而不開。善結無繩約而不可解。

謫，同謪，咎也。楗，音鍵，限門也。以上第八章讚上善若水，連擧七事。此又讚行言數閉結五事，其要妙無窮，是謂爲無爲，達無不爲之妙用。

是以聖人常善救人。故無棄人。常善救物。故無棄物。是謂襲明。

襲、音習，合也，因也。是謂襲明，乃援引古語。八十一章有謂：天之道，利而不害。聖人與天同德，猶禹之治水，稷之播穀，文王視民如傷，皆常善救人而無棄人。且至於恩及禽獸，澤及昆蟲，故常善救物，而無棄物。皆合乎天道，不獨因襲其明德而

二十八章 Chapter 28

Know the masculine; cleave to the feminine.
Be the valley for the world.
To be the valley for the world,
do not swerve from your innate nature
and return to the state of infancy.
Know the bright; keep to the dull.
Be a guide for the world.
To be a guide for the world,
follow your innate nature without changing
and return to the pre-conceptual.
Understand glory; keep to humility.
Be the valley for the world.
Innate nature completed, return to original uniqueness.

Lecture: This section clarifies how the Tao benefits from being the lesser and delineates the ways for a person to proceed. See Chapter 32, "Tao is to the world as a brook or valley is to the river or ocean." Chapter 66 says, "that which makes the river and ocean king of the hundred valleys is the ability to benefit from being lower." The message is the same: cleave to the feminine, the dull, or humility, and benefit from the lesser position. To "be the valley" or to "be a guide" indicate ways for a person to proceed. Never swerve from your innate nature, thereby bringing it to fullness, and you will be able to return to the state of infancy and the pre-conceptual, or original uniqueness. Thus, in turns, Lao-tzu describes the Tao itself, for it is so difficult to name.

When original uniqueness is divided,
It then becomes the instrumentalities.
The Sage employs them,
They then become the officers.
Thus, subtle governance shapes not.

Compare the preceeding with Chapter 32, "no matter how insignificant one's original uniqueness may be, nothing in the world can make it inferior," because it is a nucleus complete in itself. As soon as original uniqueness is divided and instrumentalities appear, the situation no longer includes only the Tao itself. Therefore the Sage employs the instrumentalities as officers, according to their capacities. If they return to original uniqueness, it may be likened to subtle governance that does not shape.

Chapter 28

器，則非若道體也，故聖人用爲官長，得分治也。若歸於樸，猶大制之不割裂也。

二十八章

知其雄。守其雌。爲天下谿。爲天下谿。常德不離。復歸於嬰兒。知其白。守其黑。爲天下式。爲天下式。常德不忒。復歸於無極。知其榮。守其辱。爲天下谷。爲天下谷。常德乃足。復歸於樸。

此皆喻道之善下，及有所歸也，與三十二章：譬道之在天下，猶川谷之於江海。六十六章：江海之所以爲百谷王者，以其善下之。同此意也，守雌及黑與辱，善下也。爲谿，及谷與式，有所歸也。常德不離不忒，乃足，故能歸於嬰兒與無極及樸也。此反復形容道體，以其爲難名也。

樸散則爲器。聖人用之。則爲官長。故大制不割。

參看三十二章。樸雖小，天下莫能臣，以其實完整也。及樸散爲

Chapter 29

二十九章

將欲取天下而爲之。吾見其不得已。天下神器。不可爲也。爲者敗之。執者失之。

神無形，器無神，神之爲器，以喻天下之不可爲，猶不可執也。

故物或行或隨。或歔或吹。或强或羸。或挫或隳。

是以聖人去甚、去奢、去泰。

挫字據河上公本，作載，義較合。六十四章謂：聖人以輔萬物之自然，而不敢爲。故任其行隨歔吹强羸載隳，不過去甚及奢與泰而已耳。

二十九章 Chapter 29

If someone strives to be the ruler of the world,
I do not see how he can succeed.
The world is a spiritual vessel which one cannot strive after.
Those who strive after it, fail.
Those who try to grasp it, lose it.

Lecture: Spirit has no shape, while a vessel has no spirit. Speaking of a vessel endowed with spirit stresses that the world is something that one can neither strive for nor grasp.

Thus it is that creatures either lead or follow, puff strongly or softly, grow powerful or weaken, decline or fall.
And therefore the Sage does away with excess, extravagance, and extremes.

Ho-shang Kung's version makes it "persevere" instead of "decline," which seems more appropriate. Chapter 64 says the Sage "assists all things to fulfill their natures, not daring to contrive any other action." He proceeds according to whether leading or following, puffing strongly or softly, growing powerful or weakening, persevering or falling, only doing away with any excess, extravagance, or extreme.

Chapter 30

三十章

以道佐人主者。不以兵强天下。其事好還。師之所處。荆棘生焉。大軍之後。必有凶年。

所謂其事好還，猶殺人者人恒殺之之意。三十一章有：佳兵者不祥之器，物或惡之，故有道者不處。四十二章有謂：强梁者，不得其死。且兵所過，凶害隨至，非獨君子不爲，且亦不忍覩也。

善有果而已。不敢以取强。果而勿矜。果而勿伐。果而勿驕。果而不得已。果而勿强。物壯則老。是謂不道。不道早已。

果，克敵致果也。謂以道强天下者。然已致果，尤不可矜，及伐與驕。至不得已時，仍勿取强，以物壯便老，猶兵强則折，非道也，不道，則早已。

三十章 Chapter 30

Those who use Tao to help the ruler
never use arms to force the world.
Such affairs tend to reverse themselves.
Nettles grow where an army camps.
After a war famine is bound to follow.

Lecture: "Such affairs tend to reverse themselves" contends that one who kills will in turn be killed. Chapter 31 says, "fine weapons are not auspicious instruments. Everything hates them. Therefore practitioners of the Tao will have nothing to do with them." Chapter 42 says, "the end of a strong one is an untimely death." Moreover, calamity follows an army wherever it goes. Not only does a good man not do such things, he cannot even bear the sight of them.

Subtly arrange the outcome and nothing more.
Do not use force.
After the outcome do not be complacent.
After the outcome do not be smug.
After the outcome do not be conceited.
Overcome only because there is no other alternative.
Overcome but do not force.
To mature is to age, and is called contra-Tao.
That which runs counter to the Tao is soon finished.

"Outcome" means to overcome an enemy. This chapter speaks of those who use Tao to strengthen the world. After receiving the expected outcome one must not be complacent, smug, or conceited. Even when there is no choice but to go to war, do not be forceful since anything that grows strong must soon decay, just as a flint knife is easily broken. Force is against Tao, and what is against Tao will soon cease to be.

三十一章 Chapter 31

Fine weapons are not auspicious instruments.
Everything hates them.
Therefore practitioners of Tao will have nothing to do with them.
In everyday life the noble man regards the left side of the host as the place of honor.
In war the right side of the commander is the place of honor.
Since weapons are inauspicious instruments, they are not the instruments of a noble man.
He uses them only when necessary, for peace and quiet are what he holds highest.
To him even a victory is not worthy of celebration.
Those who celebrate it take pleasure in the slaughter of men.
Those who take pleasure in the slaughter of men consequently cannot have their will with the world.

Lecture: The phrase "fine weapons are not auspicious instruments" has upset quiet a few commentators. Ho-shang Kung, Kuo Hsüan, and Wang Pi all used "fine" without any commentary. Later scholars made varying commentaries, replacing "fine" with "this" as being more correct, but there are several places elsewhere in the text where "this" is used to begin a sentence. It is difficult to believe that none of those is wrong, and only this is the exception. I have suspended judgment and left it the old way.

On auspicious occasions the place of honor is to the left of the host;
On inauspicious occasions the place of honor is to the right.
In the military the lesser commanders stand on the left,
While the commander-in-chief stands on the right, the same as in the etiquette of funerary rites.
When many people have been killed there is mourning, grief, and tears.
Hence, even victory is treated according to funerary rites.

"On auspicious occasions . . . the left . . . on inauspicious occasions . . . the right . . ." is according to ancient ritual. Hence the ancients when they took up arms believed it to be inauspicious, and so they used the right side. They did not even consider victory a cause for celebration because they mourned the slaughtered multitudes. That is why Chapter 69 says, "when opposing troops resist each other, the one stung by grief will be the victor."

Chapter 31

言以喪禮處之。殺人之衆。以哀悲泣之。戰勝以喪禮處之。

吉事尚左，凶事尚右，古禮也。故古之用兵，以爲凶事，亦尚右。雖勝，猶以爲不美。殺人衆，乃哀泣之。六十九章故謂：抗兵相加，哀者勝矣。

三十一章

夫佳兵者。不祥之器。物或惡之。故有道者不處。君子居則貴左。用兵則貴右。兵者不祥之器。非君子之器。不得已而用之。恬淡爲上。勝而不美。而美之者。是樂殺人。夫樂殺人者。則不可得志於天下矣。

夫佳兵不祥之器，殊欠安。而河上公葛玄與王弼本，俱作佳，未加注。後之考者，各殊，較以作唯字近理。然以夫惟冠首，以下叠見，皆未錯，惟此佳字獨訛，未之信。姑仍佳兵之舊，闕疑之爲愈。

吉事尚左。凶事尚右。偏將軍居左。上將軍居右。

三十二章 Chapter 32

Tao is always without a name.
Small as it may be in its original uniqueness,
It is inferior to no power in the world.
If a ruler can cleave to it,
All beings will pay homage to him.

Lecture: In an earlier chapter I commented on "Tao is always without a name." Because the characteristic of Tao is its purity, "original uniqueness" describes purity, though tiny as a pea. Therefore, "small as it may be . . . it is inferior to no power in the world," even the Tao. As for the line, "if a ruler can cleave to it," Chapter 39 states, "officials attained Oneness and became the orthodox of the world," because he cleaves to his own firm position, that of uprightness.

Note: In Chapter 37, "I will keep them in their places with the original uniqueness of the Nameless," expands upon the present chapter. Tao is "always without a name," and here is called "original uniqueness." Later on, "without a name" describes "uniqueness," and in the opposite sense, Tao is "everlasting Non-action." Scholars little versed in rules of literature have misplaced a punctuation mark, making the text read "always nameless original uniqueness," which is nonsense. If one nonchalantly inserts "nameless original uniqueness," then the phrase "keep them in their places with the original uniqueness of the Nameless" is backwards.

Heaven and earth mingle in harmony and a sweet liquor
rains down.
Without command from above peace and order spread
among the people.
With the genesis of the world, names appeared.
There are so many names, is it not time to stop?
Knowing when to stop is to be free from danger.
Tao is to the world as rivers and oceans are to brooks and valleys.

The *ch'i* of heaven descends, the *ch'i* of earth rises, and their intermingling becomes springtime, causing a "sweet liquor" to fall. If a ruler can cleave to the Tao, it will spontaneously spread among the people, and his government will achieve peace. "With the genesis of the world . . ." see Chapter 25: "I do not know its name. I reluctantly style it 'Tao', and if forced to, reluctantly describe it as 'great'," thereby, "names come to be." "Knowing when to stop is to be free from danger," and one will be durable. Therefore, the world is to the Tao as streams and valleys which return water are to rivers and oceans which receive it.

Chapter 32

。名亦既有。夫亦將知止。知止可以不殆。譬道之在天下。猶川谷之於江海。

天氣下降，地氣上升，天地和合自成春，故甘露從之以降。侯王自能守其貞，民亦莫之令而自均，則政得其平矣。始制，承上二十五章：吾不知其名，强字之曰道，强爲之名曰大，則有名矣。知止可以不殆，而能長久。故天下之於道，猶川谷之歸江海也。

三十二章

道常無名。樸雖小。天下莫能臣也。侯王若能守之。萬物將自賓。

道常無名，注見上。以其尙質樸，故以樸實爲喻，樸實其小如豆，故曰：雖小，天下莫能以臣視之。而況道乎。侯王若能守之。三十九章謂：侯王得一以爲天下貞。是乃守其貞也，貞，正也。賓，從也。

按：三十七章有：吾將鎭之以無名之樸。正爲此章發揮。以道常無名，喻之以樸也，旋亦以無名二字名樸，反以喻道之常無爲也。後之昧於文理者，亂將此句，以無名樸爲逗，不倫。若突然舉出無名樸在前，旋用鎭之以無名之樸，則倒置矣。

天地相合。以降甘露。民莫之令而自均。始制有名

Chapter 33

三十三章

知人者智。自知者明。勝人者有力。自勝者强。

知人雖智，何如自知之明？不然則曰：雖智大迷。勝人者，雖有其能力與智力，不如自勝者强，老氏主以柔克剛爲强，故曰：心使氣曰强。反之則曰！强梁者不得其死。

知足者富。强行者有志。不失其所者久。死而不亡者壽。

知足者不貪，不貪者，苟有已爲富矣。强行者有志，無爲無欲，非强其志者，惡可得也？死而不亡者，謂雖死而道不廢，則壽，故曰：沒身不殆。

三十三章 Chapter 33

One who knows men is intelligent;
One who knows himself has insight.
One who conquers men is strong;
One who conquers himself has steadfastness.

Lecture: Although it takes intelligence to know men, how can it compare with the insight of the man who knows himself? In other words, although the man who knows men is intelligent, he is a great fool. One who conquers men, although capable and intelligent, cannot compare to one with steadfastness who has conquered himself. Lao-tzu stresses steadfastness—or using the soft to overcome the hard—hence he says, "directing the breath *(ch'i)* by heart/mind is called steadfastness." What a contrast to "a strong one will come to an untimely end!"

One who knows sufficiency is rich.
One who pursues his objective with steadfastness has will power.
One who does not lose what he has gained is durable.
One who dies yet still remains has longevity.

One who knows sufficiency is not greedy. If one is not greedy, he will feel wealthy with what he has. "One who pursues his aim with steadfastness has will power:" certainly, how can one attain Non-action and No-desire without a firm will? "One who dies yet still remains" speaks of a man whose Tao has not perished even though the man himself is gone. This is longevity: "though his body ceases to be, he is not destroyed."

Chapter 34

三十四章

大道氾兮。其可左右。萬物恃之而生而不辭。功成不名。有衣養萬物。而不爲主。常無欲可名於小。

氾，廣也。道大且不獨無左右之可言，然上下六虛，亦一環耳。萬物恃之而不辭，謂不名及不爲主者，即十章與五十一章有所謂：生而不有，爲而不恃。以此言無欲，猶若可名其小。

萬物歸焉而不爲主。可名爲大。以其終不自爲大。故能成其大。

萬物歸焉而不爲主，可名爲大，乃無爲，結不自大，故能成其大，與六十三章同出。

三十四章 Chapter 34

The great Tao is so all pervasive, how can we tell where its right or left is?
All things depend on it for growth, and it requires nothing from them.
It accomplishes its work, but makes no claim for itself.
It clothes and feeds all, but does not control them.
Everlasting Non-desire is called "the lesser."

Lecture: "All pervasive" describes vastness and breadth. The Tao is so great that one cannot speak of left or right, up, down, or the four cardinal directions; its sphere is everywhere. Everything depends on it, but it requires nothing, neither recognition nor fealty. The same thought is expressed in chapters 10 and 51: "produce, but do not possess; act, but do not control." Non-desire includes elements which might be styled "the lesser."

That all things return to it and yet it does not control them is called "the greater."
Because it never insists on its greatness,
Its greatness becomes a reality.

The line, "all things return to it, yet it does not control them is called 'the greater'," refers to Non-action. The line, "because it never insists on its greatness, its greatness becomes a reality," expresses the same thought as Chapter 63.

Chapter 35

三十五章

執大象。天下往。往而不害安平太。樂與餌。過客止。道之出口。淡乎其無味。視之不見。聽之不足聞。用之不足既。

此章自執大象，至過客止。一節之文字，詰屈支離，且句調特殊。老子所謂，吾言甚易知，此則不類也。河上公王弼等，皆强爲之解，不知所云耳。不如闕疑，較任添蛇足之爲愈也。

三十五章 Chapter 35

The world moves toward the possessor of the great image.
Moving toward him there is no harm, only peace and order.
The passing guest pauses for sweetmeats and music.
The Tao that is uttered seems bland, even flavorless.
It does not appear noteworthy.
It does not sound worth listening to.
It has unlimited uses.

Lecture: From the beginning of this chapter up to the words, "the passing guest pauses for sweetmeats and music," the language is unusual and the sentence construction extraordinary. It does not conform with Lao-tzu's claim, "my words are very easy to understand." Ho-shang Kung, Wang Pi, et al., give rather forced explanations about which I am at a loss to comment. I feel it is better to suspend judgment to avoid overdoing things by "adding legs to a snake" (not knowing when to stop).

Chapter 36

三十六章

將欲歙之。必固張之。將欲弱之。必固强之。將欲廢之。必固興之。將欲奪之。必固與之。是謂微明。

歙，猶歛也。固，猶故也。將欲歛之，故意將其張開。至欲奪固與止，同一用意。微明，猶微妙幽明之意。此引古語，與襲明類也。

柔弱勝剛强。魚不可脫於淵。國之利器。不可以示人。

七十八章有謂：天下莫柔弱於水，而攻堅强者，莫之能勝。故謂淵深水柔，魚性雖剛强，不能脫也。可見歙張與奪，與柔能勝剛，皆用兵之奇，乃猶國之利器，不可示人。

三十六章 Chapter 36

That which would be shrunken must first be purposely stretched.
That which would be weakened must first be
purposely strengthened.
That which would be overthrown must first be purposely set up.
He who would take must first purposely give.
This is called *wei ming*.

Lecture: From "that which would be shrunken" to "he who would take," the text stresses a single functional principle. *Wei ming*, which means "wonderfully minute and obscure, yet brilliant," is an ancient saying similar in kind to *hsi ming* (see Ch. 27).

Softness and suppleness overcome hardness and strength.
Fish cannot leave the depths.
The sharpest weapons of the state cannot be displayed.

Chapter 78 states, "nothing in the world is softer and more supple than water, yet for attacking the hard and strong, nothing can match it." No matter how strong a fish may be, it cannot escape the ocean filled with soft, supple water. Stretching in order to shrink, giving so as to gain, weakness overcoming strength, all indicate unorthodox strategy. Just so, a nation must not display its most potent weapons.

Chapter 37

三十七章

道常無名。而無不爲。侯王若能守之。萬物將自化。化而欲作。吾將鎮之以無名之樸。夫亦將無欲。不欲以靜。天下將自定。

此章與前三十二章，用意與句調，俱近似。惟前章以樸喻道，此章以道之無名名樸，二則猶一也。考之者，謬謂前章乃道常無名樸，與此並觀，可以自見矣。此謂萬物化而欲有作，故欲以無名之樸鎮之，亦將無欲。雖不欲，其以靜，則天下亦將自定，故曰道常無名，而無不爲矣。

三十七章 Chapter 37

Tao is always without a name,
Yet there is nothing it does not do.
If a ruler can cleave to it,
All beings will eventually change by themselves.
After this change, when they desire to act,
He will keep them in their places with the original uniqueness of the Nameless.
Eventually there will be Non-desire.
If no desires, then serenity,
And eventually the world will settle itself by itself.

Lecture: This chapter is the same as Chapter 32, except that, in the earlier chapter "original uniqueness" characterizes Tao, while in this chapter it describes the namelessness of Tao. Thus the two chapters form a unity. Some commentators have mistakenly taken the earlier chapter to read, "Tao is forever nameless original uniqueness," but from this chapter the entire picure is self-evident. When all beings change and they desire to act, then the ruler uses the "original uniqueness of the Nameless" to curb them. Eventually there will be Non-desire. Having no desires will bring serenity, and eventually the world will also naturally settle down. Hence, "the Tao is always without a name, yet there is nothing it does not do."

下篇 Part 2

三十八章 Chapter 38

Superior Teh does not reveal its Teh, thereby retaining it.
Inferior Teh cannot rid itself of the appearance of Teh,
and thereby loses it.
Superior Teh practices Non-action and has no private ends to serve.
Inferior Teh both acts and has private ends to serve.
Superior humanism *(jen)* acts but has no private ends to serve.
Superior justice *(yi)* both acts and has private ends to serve.
Superior etiquette *(li)* not only acts but, getting no response,
tries to enforce its will with raised fists.
Thus, if Tao is lost, Teh appears.
If Teh is lost, humanism appears.
If humanism is lost, justice appears.
If justice is lost, etiquette appears.
When conscience and honesty wear thin,
Etiquette is the beginning of strife.

Lecture: Concerning "if Tao is lost, Teh appears," Tao and Teh cannot be parted, nor can *yin* and *yang*, nor can male and female. If they could be separated, what would become of nature, of the human race? Superior Teh and inferior Teh are as different as natural and unnatural. Humanism and justice naturally have a difference: the basis of justice is right and wrong. When superior etiquette acts but gets no response, it goes to the extreme of physical violence, so distant from the Tao. That is why "when conscience and honesty wear thin, etiquette is the beginning of strife."

As to prescience, it is merely a blossom of Tao, and the beginnings of stupidity.
That is why the truly cultivated man takes generosity for his location, and does not dwell on meanness;
Focuses on the fruit and does not dwell on the blossom.
So he avoids the one and chooses the other.

Chapter 26 states, "not daring to be first, one can lead all 'instruments'," so Lao-tzu does not consider the foreknowledge of events a serious matter. Those who are prescient compete among themselves to be first, much as the stupid blithely undertake matters of consequence, and are the equivalent of a mere blossom of the Tao. One must treat such desires by "keeping them in their places with the original uniqueness of the Nameless." One must seriously respect the fruit, take generosity for his locus, and "not dwell on the blossom." One must assiduously avoid 'that' which is merely a small instrument, and cleave to 'this', into which Tao will naturally transform 'that'.

Chapter 38

前識者。道之華。而愚之始。是以大丈夫處其厚。不居其薄。處其實。不居其華。故去彼取此。

六十七章謂：不敢爲天下先，故能成器長。是以不重前識，識競人先，猶道發華耳，亦愚者之始事也。必欲鎮之以無名之樸，崇其實，處其厚，不居其華，去彼所成器小，守此以道自化。

三十八章

上德不德。是以有德。下德不失德。是以無德。上德無爲。而無以爲。下德爲之。而有以爲。上仁爲之。而無以爲。上義爲之。而有以爲。上禮爲之。而莫之應。則攘臂而扔之。故失道而後德。失德而後仁。失仁而後義。失義而後禮。夫禮者。忠信之薄。而亂之首。

失道而德，道之與德，不可離也，猶陰之與陽，與男之與女也。可離，則不得其爲天，爲人也。上德與下德，自然與反自然之不同。仁與義自有差別，上義爲之，以有是非也。上禮爲之，而莫之應，甚至待其攘臂引之，乃失道矣。故謂之忠信之薄，而亂之首耳。扔，音仍，引也。

三十九章 Chapter 39

In times past Oneness appeared in the following pattern:
The heavens attained Oneness and became clear;
The earth attained Oneness and settled;
The spirits attained Oneness and became numinous;
Valleys attained Oneness and became reproductive;
All things attained Oneness and became alive;
Kings and officials attained Oneness and became the orthodox of the world.

Lecture: Chapter 22 says, "the Sage embraces the Oneness of the Tao and becomes a guide for the whole world." Later, in Chapter 28, it says, "to be a guide for the world, follow your innate nature without changing." Here, to attain Oneness is to become clear, settled, numinous, filled, reproductive, and orthodox, which all illustrates "the Sage embraces the Oneness of the Tao."

In the heavens, that which is not clear eventually settles.
On the earth, that which does not settle dissipates.
Spirits which are not numinous disappear.
Valleys not filled will dry up.
Creatures that do not reproduce become extinct.
Kings and officials, if not honored and esteemed, will fall.

"The heavens attained Oneness and became clear" refers to *ch'i* or Tao. If the heavens were not in a state of Oneness, they would not be clear, they would be turgid. That which is turgid has weight, which is not the quality of the heavens, but of the earth. Therefore, "in the heavens, that which is not clear eventually settles." This is obvious. The sense of the text harmonizes with "the Sage embraces the Oneness of Tao" and ". . . follow your innate nature without changing." "(The) not numinous disappear" and "(the) not filled dry up" are also in accord with this same idea. *Ch'i* fills the valleys. Without *ch'i* the valleys become arid.

Hence the honorable takes the humble as its trunk.
The high takes the low as its foundation.
That is why officials call themselves the lonely, the hubless.
This is taking the humble for the trunk, is it not?
Therefore, it is better to consider the vacancy of the vehicle rather than its appearance.
Do not desire to be as shiny and attractive as fine jade.
Be as ordinary as stone.

The Ho-shang Kung edition says, "the analogy 'the lonely, the hubless' describes the inability to be like a hub, the center for converging spokes." The text continues, explaining "therefore it is better to consider the vacancy of the vehicle rather than its appearance." This reference to a hub is the same as in Chapter 11: "thirty spokes converge at a single hub: it is the vacancy that begets the vehicle's usefulness." Wang Pi changes 'hubless' to read 'grainless', which in this context makes no sense at all. He uses 'carriage' instead of 'vehicle', and he uses 'hardness' in place of 'ordinary'. His efforts are not as well directed as those of Ho-shang Kung, who goes on to say that without a foundation or a trunk neither the high nor the honorable can succeed; that officials who are lonely cannot become 'hubs'; and that to be 'shiny and attractive' puts a premium on rarity, while the 'ordinary' is so commonplace that it is quite inexpensive and available.

Chapter 39

也。明矣。此與聖人抱一常德不忒一意也。餘如發泄歇絕，則滅則蹶，皆同此意。惟谷得氣以盈，無氣則亦枯竭焉。

故貴以賤爲本。高以下爲基。是以侯王自謂孤寡不轂。此非以賤爲本邪非乎。故致數車無車。不欲琭琭如玉。落落如石。

河上公本作：孤寡不轂，謂以轂喻不能如車轂，爲衆輻所湊，且下文接故致數車無車，此與十一章：三十輻共一轂，當其無車之用。同此轂也。王弼作不穀，上下文俱無此意。且車字作輿，落落作珞珞，俱不及河上公本爲是。謂高貴者無基本不成，侯王孤寡，則不成其爲轂，琭琭稀少而貴，落落多且賤矣。

三十九章

昔之得一者。天得一以清。地得一以寧。神得一以靈。谷得一以盈。萬物得一以生。侯王得一以爲天下貞。

二十二章謂：聖人抱一爲天下式。又曰：爲天下式，常德不忒。所謂得一以淸，以寧，以靈，以盈，以生，以貞者，此六者，亦猶聖人抱一之意而已。

天無以清。將恐裂。地無以寧。將恐發。神無以靈。將恐歇。谷無以盈。將恐竭。萬物無以生。將恐滅。侯王無以貴高。將恐蹶。

天得一以淸者，氣也，道也；天如不得一，則不淸，不淸卽是濁，濁則重，重濁，非天，乃成地也，故謂：天不得淸將恐其分裂

Chapter 40

四十章

反者道之動。弱者道之用。天下萬物生於有。有生於無。

二十五章言：道大，大曰逝，逝曰遠，遠曰反。不反者，窮也，竭也。故反者，道之動力也，在天尚陰，在地尚柔，在人尚母及嬰兒，在物尚水，此皆爲道之用。首章謂：無名天地之始，有名萬物之母。萬物母，天地始，乃生於混一之氣，天得一以淸，地得一以寧，是爲一生二。天地相合，以降甘露，是爲沖和之氣，乃二生三也，三生萬物，是爲有生於無。

四十章 Chapter 40

Tao moves in cycles;
Tao functions through softness.
All is born of something;
Something is born of nothing.

Lecture: Describing the greatness of Tao Chapter 25 says, " 'great' can be described as going ever onward. 'Going ever onward' can be described as going far. 'Going far' can be described as returning." That which does not return is worn out, finished. Cyclical return gives Tao motion. The feminine principle *(yin)* is the focus of reference for heaven, softness is the reference point for earth, the mother and infant form the reference for mankind, water is the reference in nature. Each has connection with the function of Tao. The first chapter states, "that which has no name is the origin of heaven and earth; that which has a name is the Mother of all things." Both the "Mother" of all things and the "origin" of heaven and earth result from *ch'i* attaining Oneness, the same way "the heavens attained Oneness and became clear; the earth attained Oneness and settled." This illustrates "unity gives birth to duality." When "heaven and earth mingle in harmony and a sweet liquor rains down," nature reproduces and "duality gives birth to trinity, and trinity gives birth to all things." Therefore, "something is born of nothing."

四十一章 Chapter 41

When a superior scholar hears the Tao
he tirelessly practices it.
When a middling scholar hears the Tao,
sometimes he follows it
and sometimes he forgets it.
When a piddling scholar hears the Tao
he laughs loudly at it.
Without his laughter it would not be worthy of being Tao,
Hence the sayings:
"One who understands the Tao seems benighted;
One who progresses toward the Tao seems to regress;
One who is in accord with Tao seems tied in knots."

Lecture: One who hears the Tao and can practice it vigorously is a "superior scholar." One who hears it but only practices it half-heartedly because of doubts and lack of confidence is a "middling scholar." One who hears it and breaks out in loud laughter is a "piddling scholar." The latter is completely in the dark about Tao and his ignorance prompts the words, "without his laughter it would not be worthy of being Tao." Old adages reflect this: one who understands Tao seems benighted, progress seems like regress, and to be in accord seems to be tied in knots. The old adages are similar to the saying, "great wisdom seems like stupidity," which piddling scholars understand even less, precisely the reason they give contrary reactions.

Great Teh seems like a valley.
The completely immaculate seems disgraced.
The thoroughly virtuous seems insufficient.
Established morality seems a conspiracy.
True characteristics seem submerged.
A great square has no corners.
A great instrument is completed late.
A great sound comes from a small noise.

A great form has no shape.
Tao is hidden and nameless,
Yet wonderfully, Tao guarantees that all things are fulfilled.

The first five sentences are related to the saying "one who understands Tao seems benighted." If something seems like nothing, and a great square seems round, then may not a circle have corners? The completion of a great instrument definitely takes a long time. A great sound certainly is present in a tiny, tiny noise. A great form essentially has no shape. Therefore, "Tao is hidden and nameless" describes these sentences. And then Tao, bailing out these bankruptcies, as it were, wonderfully sees that all things are fulfilled.

Chapter 41

自若谷至若渝五句，與明道若昧意同，有若無，大方，猶圓也，圓安能有隅?器大當然成之晚也。大音直當是希小之聲，大象直當是無形，此之謂道隱於無名也。然而惟道，一任假貸，且善其成也。

四十一章

上士聞道。勤而行之。中士聞道。若存若亡。下士聞道。大笑之。不笑不足以爲道。故建言有之。明道若昧。進道若退。夷道若纇。

聞道能力行者，上士也；疑信參半者，中士也；聞而大笑者，下士也，以其昧於道也。故謂不笑不足以爲道。建，立也。纇，絲之結節也。故立言者，有謂明道若昧，進若退，夷若纇，此猶謂大智若愚，尤非下士所能知也，是以得其反耳。

大德若谷。大白若辱。廣德若不足。建德若偷。質眞若渝。大方無隅。大器晩成。大音希聲。大象無形。道隱無名。夫唯道。善貸且成。

四十二章 Chapter 42

Tao gives birth to unity, unity gives birth to duality, duality gives birth to trinity, and trinity gives birth to all things.
All things are wrapped by *yin* and contain *yang*, and their pulsing *ch'i*s marry.
That which men abominate, the lonely, the hubless, their leaders take as names.
Thus does one either benefit from a loss or lose from a benefit.

Lecture: Yang corresponds to ⚊. When *yang* peaks, *yin* begins. *Yin* corresponds to ⚋. These lines inspire the words, "unity gives birth to duality." In the *Book of Change yin-yang* is symbolized ⚍. When *yin* peaks, *yang* begins, and this is "returning" (cyclical, circulating), so the "duality" of the *yin* gives birth to ⚍ or "trinity." In the *Book of Change yang* is one solid line (⚊), but it is in fact made up of three internal sections ▪▪▪ , so the "duality" of the *yin* giving birth to "trinity" means *yin* (⚋) transforms into ▪▪▪ . This is the "interplay" of *yin-yang* or the "marriage" of heaven and earth. "And trinity gives birth to all things," which in turn reproduce. This is "the *ch'i*s of heaven and earth mingle: nature quickens," and "male and female unite: nature impregnates." As for "all things are wrapped by *yin* and contain *yang*," *yin* takes the external shape and *yang* is that contained in the middle, yet one-third of it is shaped ▪▪▪ .* "Their pulsing *ch'i*s marry" is the circulating current of *ch'i* produced alternately by *yin* and *yang*. This is what the *Book of Change* calls the processes of "transfer" and "transformation." According to these processes, all things are born of the earth, they are "wrapped by *yin*," hence *yin* and softness dominate the earth. Lao-tzu borrows this viewpoint from the *Book of Change*, and proclaims that (ancient Chinese) rulers called themselves "the lonely." Even though men dislike loneliness and believe it a "loss", rulers call themselves "lonely," since they are cautious too much benefit will come their way. "Thus does one either benefit from a loss or lose from a benefit."

What other people teach, I also teach.
"The end of a strong one is an untimely death."
I will take this as a precept to teach proper behavior.

This seems to say what I have taught is just like that of others. "A strong one" means a strong horizontal or crossing force, as when the straightness of a column is crossed by a beam. A strong cross-force overdoes the *yang* and the hard, and falls out of harmony with the upward thrusting *ch'i*. "The stiff and hard are the moribund ones," describes this situation, which will result in an untimely death. According to the *Shuo Wen* (the earliest dictionary of Chinese, compiled in the second century, A.D.), "proper behavior means the everyday, household rules of good behavior." Lao-tzu is the proponent of *yin* and softness, the precise contrary of strength, therefore, he "chooses the former" and teaches proper behavior.

* 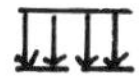  (this happens at the same time, i.e. it is mutual), giving,  which is represented as  .

Chapter 42

以爲損，而王公偏自稱孤寡，是虞其過益也，此卽或損之而益，或益之而損之謂也。

人之所教。我亦教之。强梁者不得其死。吾將以爲教父。

似謂我之所教，亦猶人也，强梁者，卽强橫也，以柱直，而梁橫耳。强橫者過用陽剛，而失冲和之氣，此所謂：剛强者死之徒也，故謂不得其死。父，說文：矩也，謂家長率教以矩耳。老氏主陰與柔，强梁適與之相反，故將以取此，爲教之矩云爾。

四十二章

道生一。一生二。二生三。三生萬物。萬物負陰而抱陽。沖氣以爲和。人之所惡。唯孤寡不穀。而王公以爲稱。故物或損之而益。或益之而損

陽是⚊，陽極而陰生。陰是⚋，是之謂一而生二，卽在易卦陰陽作⚏，陰極而陽生之謂來復，故謂之陰二而生此⚏三也。在易卦，陽⚊而其中包含爲三，如☷形，此爲陰二生三，亦卽陰⚋，變易作☷也。是之謂陰陽交錯，卽天地交泰也，由三生萬物，乃化成也，此之謂天地絪緼，萬物化醇，男女構精，萬物化生。負陰而抱陽者，卽陰成形於外，而中間所抱者，猶有三之一爲☷形者，陽也。沖氣以爲和者，卽陰陽相生之沖和氣也，乃易之所謂交易變易之道。此道也，以萬物皆由地生，是爲負陰，故以陰與柔主之。此老氏所取於易之道也，故謂王公以孤寡爲稱，人惡孤寡

Chapter 43

四十三章

天下之至柔。馳騁天下之至堅。無有入無間。吾是以知無爲之有益。不言之教。無爲之益。天下希及之。

天下之至柔者，猶風與水也。及其力之積也，排山倒海，可以馳騁天下之至堅，極其微也。以無有入無間，淺言其漸也。如風過銅摩，水滴石穿，進而言氣如滲潤透達，眞理俱著，持久自知。此無爲之益，猶不言之教，天下希及之。

四十三章 Chapter 43

The softest in the world overcomes the strongest, just as a rider controls his galloping steed.
The insubstantial can penetrate where there is no opening.
Because of that I know the benefit of Non-action.
Few in the world attain wordless teaching and the benefit of Non-action.

Lecture: Water and wind are among the softest things in the world, but when their force is concentrated, it is enough to topple mountains and overturn the sea. "Just as a rider controls his galloping steed," the strongest things in the world are overcome. In its minutest form, softness allows the insubstantial to penetrate where there is no opening. The wind erodes copper or dripping water bores through stone in the same way. By extending this description we can include *ch'i* with its ability to permeate and moisten everywhere. These are all examples of natural phenomena. If one holds to this precept he will gradually and naturally discover just how true it is. This, then, is a benefit of Non-action, as is wordless teaching, but few in the world can attain it.

Chapter 44

四十四章

名與身孰親。身與貨孰多。得與亡孰病。是故甚愛必大費。多藏必厚亡。知足不辱。知止不殆。可以長久。

若甚愛名與貨，則身必大有所耗費。試問孰爲得失，知多藏必厚亡。能知足知止，可免乎辱與殆，能久長矣。

四十四章 Chapter 44

Which is dearer, fame or health?
Which is worth more, health or wealth?
Which is more harmful, gain or loss?
Hence, excessive love finally exacts its price.
The certain consequence of proud ownership is ruin.
To know sufficiency is to be blameless.
Knowing when to stop avoids danger.
Thereby one can be durable.

Lecture: To have excessive love of fame and possessions will certainly result in a great loss of health. The text raises the question: what is gain and loss? Knowing that proud ownership inevitably preceeds an unbearable loss brings on understanding of what sufficiency is and when to stop, avoiding both shame and danger and resulting in durability.

Chapter 45

四十五章

大成若缺。其用不弊。大盈若沖。其用不窮。大直若屈。大巧若拙。大辯若訥。躁勝寒。靜勝熱。淸靜爲天下正。

自若缺以至於若訥七句，其意不出乎有若無，實若虛耳。寒與熱，皆可以相反而勝之，故天下雖煩囂，可以淸靜正之也。

四十五章 Chapter 45

The greatest accomplishment seems unfinished,
yet its applications are endless.
The greatest fullness seems empty,
yet its applications are never exhausted.
The greatest skill seems crude.
The greatest eloquence seems stuttering.
Activity overcomes cold.
Tranquility overcomes heat.
Peace and quiet is the true path in the world.

Lecture: The first five sentences are parallel to "something seems like nothing" and "the substantial seems insubstantial." Both cold and heat can be overcome by their opposites. Therefore, no matter how confused and noisy the world is, it can be set aright by peace and quiet.

Chapter 46

四十六章

天下有道。卻走馬以糞。天下無道。戎馬生於郊。禍莫大於不知足。咎莫大於欲得。故知足之足。常足矣。

天下有道，知足而已，糞其田，以卻走馬耳；反之，禍莫大焉。此承上章之意，知足常足矣。

四十六章 Chapter 46

When Tao prevails in the world,
stray horses are kept away from tilled fields.
When Tao does not prevail in the world,
warhorses breed in fields grown wild.
No disaster is greater than not knowing what is sufficient.
No crime is greater than avarice.
One who knows sufficiency will always have enough.

Lecture: When Tao prevails in the world, everyone knows what is enough. The fields are cultivated and horses chased out. However, "no disaster is greater . . .," etc. This chapter continues the idea expressed in a previous chapter that to know what is enough is always to have enough.

Chapter 47

四十七章

不出戶。知天下。不闚牖。見天道。其出彌遠。其知彌少。是以聖人不行而知。不見而名。不爲而成。

不出戶，以近而測知天下；不闚牖，以理達而天道自見。故謂出彌遠，而知彌少也。是以聖人不行而知，不見而名，不爲而成。下文便申之曰：無爲而無不爲也。

四十七章 Chapter 47

Without leaving his door one can understand the world.
Without glancing out the window one can see the Tao of heaven.
The further one travels the less one knows.
That is why the Sage does not travel and yet understands,
Does not look and yet names,
Does not act and yet completes.

Lecture: Without leaving one's door one can take what is available to use as a model to understand the world. Without glancing out the window one can let reason go forth until the Tao is naturally visible. That is the reason for saying, "the further one travels the less one knows." That is also why the Sage "does not travel and yet understands, does not look and yet names, does not act and yet completes." The following chapter expands on this theme: "Non-action, yet there is nothing left undone."

Chapter 48

四十八章

爲學日益。爲道日損。損之又損。以至於無爲。無爲而無不爲。取天下常以無事。及其有事。不足以取天下。

爲學者欲其日益也，爲道反爾，日欲其損，損之又損，至於無爲，無爲却無不爲，取天下猶然也。反之者，畔道也，畔道不足以取天下。

四十八章 Chapter 48

In pursuing knowledge, one accumulates daily.
In practicing Tao, one loses daily.
Lose and lose and lose, until one reaches Non-action.
Non-action, yet there is nothing left undone.
To win the world one must not act for gain.
If one acts for gain, one will not be able to win the world.

Lecture: Those pursuing knowledge want to add to it each day. In contrast, practitioners of Tao desire to reduce desire, "lose and lose and lose," until they reach the state of Non-action. Non-action, yet nothing is left undone. It is the same for those wishing to win over the world. Those who act, rebel against the Tao. Those who rebel against the Tao lack the means to win over the world.

Chapter 49

四十九章

聖人無常心。以百姓心為心。善者吾善之。不善者吾亦善之。德善。信者。吾信之。不信者。吾亦信之。德信。聖人在天下。歙歙為。天下渾其心。聖人皆孩之。

聖人渾一百姓之心為常心，故無善無不善，無信無不信，亦皆以孩視之也，此乃聖人歙歙為天下者也。歙歙，猶斂氣息貌。

四十九章 Chapter 49

The Sage is without a set mind.
He makes the mind of the people his own.
I am kind to the kind.
I am also kind to the unkind.
Thus kindness is attained.
I believe those who believe.
I believe also those who do not believe.
Thus faith is attained.
The Sage, when in the midst of the worldly, does it calmly and slowly, and his mind merges with the world.
The Sage treats everyone as his children.

Lecture: The Sage is determined only to merge his mind with the mind of the common people. To him, there is no "kind" or "unkind," no "faithful" or "unfaithful." Therefore, he regards everybody as his own children, and does it calmly and slowly as he takes care of the world. "Does it calmly and slowly" describes breathing with composure.

Chapter 50

五十章

出生入死。生之徒十有三。死之徒十有三。人之生。動之死地。亦十有三。夫何故。以其生生之厚。蓋聞善攝生者。陸行不遇兕虎。入軍不被甲兵。兕無所投其角。虎無所措其爪。兵無所容其刄。夫何故。以其無死地。

出生入死之地，如行軍，生之徒與死之徒，可能性，十各居其三。又人之生，動之死地，如自生卽自滅者，亦十居其三。以其生生之厚，生者較死者居多。與善攝生者，絕對不死，則大異，以其爲無爲，猶赤子全其天德，無死機也。此章與下文五十五章，可以參看。

五十章 Chapter 50

In circumstances of life-and-death, the chances of living are three out of ten, the chances of dying are three out of ten.
In ordinary living conditions, where activity is the province of death, the chances are also three in ten.
Why is this so?
Because of the propagative force of the life principle.
It is said that those who cultivate the life principle can travel without encountering a tiger or wild buffalo;
In battle, no weapon can penetrate their armor.
The wild buffalo's horns find nothing to gore, the tiger's claws nothing to flay, and weapons find no place for their points to penetrate.
Why is this so?
Because, for them, there is no province of death.

Lecture: In a life-and-death situation, such as battle, the possibilities of living or dying are thirty per cent. Moreover, in ordinary living conditions where Activity is the province of death, one lives or dies of his own doing. Here also the probabilities are thirty per cent. Because of the propagative force of the life principle, there are more who live than die. Those who cultivate the life principle do not meet death. The great difference is that they practice Non-action, like an infant whose vigor of sprouting life presents no opportunity for death to enter. I suggest a comparative study of this chapter and Chapter 55.

Chapter 51

五十一章

道生之。德畜之。物形之。勢成之。是以萬物莫不尊道而貴德。道之尊。德之貴。夫莫之命。而常自然。故道生之。德畜之。長之育之。亭之毒之。養之覆之。生而不有。爲而不恃。長而不宰。是謂元德。

道德之生畜，使物勢形成者，萬物除人以外，何以知其可尊貴也？此老氏之意也。且申之曰：莫之命令，純任自然耳。生畜長育，亭毒養覆，悉盡其德之所致。既不以爲有，又不以爲恃，主長而不主宰殺者，乃德之長也。

五十一章 Chapter 51

Tao propagates life; Teh provides fecundity;
species shapes life; affinity brings to completion.
That is why all living things revere Tao and kneel down to Teh.
Tao inspires reverence and Teh inspires awe because they give
no commands and yet nature continues on and on.
Thus Tao creates life, and Teh conceives, grows, fosters,
shelters, comforts, nurtures, and protects it.
Producing but not possessing,
Acting but not controlling,
Growing but not slaughtering,
These are Mysterious Teh.

Lecture: The creativity of Tao and the fecundity of Teh cause species to take shape and affinity brings all to completion. How can creatures other than men know to revere and value Tao and Teh? Yet this is Lao-tzu's claim? He emphasizes it, saying "no command is given" and each naturally performs its duties. Creating, conceiving, growing, fostering, sheltering, comforting, nurturing, and protecting tax fecund Teh to the utmost. It neither possesses nor controls. It governs growth but does not govern slaughter. Indeed, Teh has always been thus.

Chapter 52

五十二章

天下有始。以爲天下母。既得其母。以知其子。既知其子。復守其母。沒身不殆。塞其兌。閉其門。終身不勤。開其兌。濟其事。終身不救。見小曰明。守柔曰强。用其光。復歸其明。無遺身殃。是爲習常。

母爲元牝，已詳見一與四及六二章，可參之。兌在易爲說爲口，閉其門，猶緘其口，而不用勤也。若開口以濟事，則致終其身之不救。故曰：見小反謂明，守弱反爲强，能用其光，即復歸其明者，無遺身之殃，此習常之道也。習常，亦援古語耳。

五十二章 Chapter 52

The beginning of the world may be called the Mother of the world.
Once we discover the Mother, we can know the children.
Once we know the children, we should return and cleave to the mother.
Even though the body may die, there is no danger.
Close the mouth, shut the door, and to the end of life do not strain.
Open the mouth, increase involvements, and be helpless to the end of life.
To value the lesser is enlightenment.
To cleave to the gentle is steadfastness.
Use bright intellect, but return to enlightenment.
Do not ask for trouble.
This is "practicing longevity."

Lecture: "Mother" is the Mysterious Female. This idea first appears in Chapters 1, 4, and 6, which the reader should re-examine at this point. "Mouth" is related to the *tui* hexagram ("speaking" or "mouth") in the *Book of Change.* To "close the door" is like sealing the mouth shut, yet not using force. If one opens the mouth and actively pursues involvements, then one will be helpless to death. Hence, regarding the lesser is contrarily called "enlightenment;" cleaving to the gentle is contrarily called "steadfastness." Those who can use bright intellect and yet return to enlightenment will not bring trouble on themselves. This is "practicing longevity," an ancient phrase.

Chapter 53

五十三章

使我介然有知。行於大道。唯施是畏。大道甚夷。而民好徑。朝甚除。田甚蕪。倉甚虛。服文綵。帶利劍。厭飲食。財貨有餘。是謂盜夸。非道也哉。

大道甚平，而民不行，偏由小徑，故我雖有大智，行施爲於大道中，是亦可畏也。朝廷雖甚潔除，而田畝荒蕪，倉廩甚虛，而被服文綵，帶利劍，而饜飲食，財貨有餘，是悉爲盜夸眩，非合乎道也。

五十三章 Chapter 53

I have cause to know that, though I possess great wisdom,
To preach it while traveling on a highway is dangerous.
Though the highway is smooth and straight,
The common people prefer byways.
The ruler's court is well tended, but the fields are neglected.
The granaries are empty, but garments are gorgeous.
Men carry sharp swords, but food and drink satiate them.
There is a surplus of money and merchandise,
"temptation for bandits."
Alas, it is not Tao.

Lecture: Although the highway is very smooth and level the common people do not use it, preferring the byways instead. Hence, although I have great wisdom, spreading the Tao from the middle of the main road is potentially dangerous. Although the ruler's court is immaculately clean, yet fields are deserted and have gone to seed. Even though barn and silo are empty, yet "garments are gorgeous." Men carry sharp swords, yet glut themselves with food and drink. "There is a surplus of money and merchandise," which offers an irresistible temptation for bandits. None of these harmonizes with Tao.

Chapter 54

五十四章

善建者不拔。善抱者不脫。子孫以祭祀不輟。修之於身。其德乃眞。修之於家。其德乃餘。修之於鄉。其德乃長。修之於國。其德乃豐。修之於天下。其德乃普。故以身觀身。以家觀家。以鄉觀鄉。以國觀國。以天下觀天下。吾何以知天下然哉。以此。

善建不拔，善抱不脫，語氣過强，出乎老子，奇哉！修身以達乎子孫，祭祀不輟，廣之而達乎天下，此非有爲乎？似不合老氏之旨，姑闕如不加注焉。

五十四章 Chapter 54

The well established cannot be uprooted.
The well embraced cannot be lost.
Descendants will continue ancestral sacrifices for generations without end.
Cultivate (Tao) personally, and its Teh will become real.
Cultivate (Tao) in the family, and Teh will become abundant.
Cultivate (Tao) in the community, and Teh will have an enduring effect.
Cultivate (Tao) in the nation and Teh will flourish.
Cultivate (Tao) in the world and Teh will become ubiquitous.
Hence, judge a person as a person, a family as a family, a community as a community, a nation as a nation, the world as a world.
How do I know about the world?
By this.

Lecture: The language in "the well established cannot be uprooted. The well embraced cannot be lost," is too forceful for Lao-tzu. To cultivate oneself to insure that ancestral sacrifice will continue unbroken, then expanding this model to include the whole world smacks of action. This chapter is discordant with the teachings of Lao-tzu. Therefore, I leave it without further comment.

五十五章

Chapter 55

Measure the fullness of one's virtue (Teh) against an infant's:
Neither scorpion nor snake will attack it,
Nor does the tiger maul it,
Nor do birds of prey clutch it.
Its bones are pliable and sinews soft,
Yet its grip is firm.
It does not know the union of male and female,
Yet its reproductive organ is fully formed;
Its essence is whole.*
It can cry all day without getting hoarse;
This is total harmony.
To know harmony is constancy.
To know constancy is enlightening.
That which is beneficial to life is auspicious.
To direct *ch'i* by heart is steadfastness (strength).
Things mature and then decay.
This is contra-Tao.
That which runs counter to the Tao is soon finished.

Lecture: This chapter praises the fullness of an infant's virtue (Teh): its undissipated vital juices and its unimpaired harmony. This is based on reality and is not empty words. Constancy will eventually disappear without harmony; a real understanding of harmony brings constancy. Those who lose constancy also lose the requisite for wisdom, since to know constancy is enlightening. That which is harmful to life is inauspicious, just as that which is beneficial to life constitutes the auspicious. Weaklings who can mobilize *ch'i* by heart will inevitably become strong. Although Lao-tzu generally disapproves of the auspicious and the strong, he maintains that the ordinary person cannot become "auspicious" and "strong" as based on an infant's undissipated vital juices and unimpaired harmony. On the contrary, "things mature and then decay. This is contra-Tao. That which runs counter to the Tao is soon finished." The text re-emphasizes these lines which appeared in Chapter 30.

Note: "Its bones are pliable and sinews soft" contrasts with a line from Chapter 3: "strengthen the bones." The infant is pliable and soft, because it has not yet grown. The meaning of "strengthen the bones" corresponds to the lines "that which benefits life" and "to direct *ch'i* by heart is called steadfastness (strength)." This is the proper way for the Sage to educate mankind. Mobilize the spermic essence *(ching)* to supplement the bone marrow and the bones are strengthened. This is the method to remedy pre-natal deficiency.

* *Translator's Note:* This means that an infant has not yet known the union of male and female, and therefore has never known loss or imperfection.

Chapter 55

虎不以爪按拏之。䘒，小兒陰也。作，造也。謂赤子以牝牡未合，無所毀損耳。嗄，聲不變也。

按：此節言骨弱筋柔，與上之三章，强其骨，則又一事也。此謂赤子之柔弱，尚未長足，謂强其骨者，正與此節益生曰祥，心使氣曰强，同一意也，此乃聖人教人之治道也。塡精補髓，而使骨强也，此正挽救先天之道也。

五十五章

含德之厚。比於赤子。蜂蠆虺蛇不螫。猛虎不據。攫鳥不搏。骨弱筋柔而握固。未知牝牡之合。而峻作。精之至也。終日號而不嗄。和之至也。知和曰常。知常曰明。益生曰祥。心使氣曰强。物壯則老。謂之不道。不道早已。

此節贊赤子含德之厚，至精至和，純係寫實，非虛構也。不和便致失常，故知和爲常耳。失常者不足爲明智，故知常爲明耳。損其生者爲不祥，故以益生爲祥。能以心行氣者，雖柔必强。然祥之與强，皆老氏素不稱許，但由赤子之至精至和，進而言之，稱此祥之與强者，乃非常人之所能也。反此者，物壯則老矣，此已見三十章，擧而重言之。螫，音釋，螫蟲之尾，行毒也。據，謂

Chapter 56

五十六章

知者不言。言者不知。塞其兌。閉其門。挫其銳。解其紛。和其光。同其塵。是謂元同。故不可得而親。不可得而疏。不可得而利。不可得而害。不可得而貴。不可得而賤。故為天下貴。

老子嘗重言而疊舉，於此章筆法，見知其用意，豈偶然也？不可視為錯簡。吾於老子亦可以一言以蔽之，曰：思超塵，是以異於常人也，欲知其言而行之，五百言亦已足矣，其費五千言者，乃丁寧之意已耳，知者不言，言者不知，塞其兌，以至於同塵，是謂元同。元同，亦古諺也，其所不同者，意欲超塵耳，人不得親疏而貴賤之，是以為貴也。

五十六章 Chapter 56

One who knows does not speak.
One who speaks does not know.
Close the mouth.
Shut the door.
Blunt the sharp edge.
Untie the knot.
Harmonize with others' light.
Merge with the mundane world.
This is "mysterious assimilation."
When one acquires it,
One neither is familiar with it nor escapes it,
Neither takes advantage of it nor harms it,
Neither increases it nor cheapens it.
Therefore, it is the most precious thing in the world.

Lecture: Lao-tzu often ruminates, repeating himself. How can this chapter be accidental? Its purpose is evident. This chapter is also not the result of misplaced bamboo slips. I sum up my opinion of Lao-tzu in a single line: his thoughts soar high above the mundane, setting him apart from ordinary mortals. Five hundred characters would give ample instruction to one who wishes to learn and practice Lao-tzu's thought. He wasted five thousand characters only to repeat and stress. The first eight sentences describe "mysterious assimilation." "Mysterious assimilation" is an ancient phrase. Lao-tzu differs from others in the way his thoughts long to transcend the earthbound. Man can neither be familiar with it nor escape it, therefore he can neither increase nor cheapen its value. That makes it precious.

Chapter 57

五十七章

以正治國。以奇用兵。以無事取天下。吾何以知其然哉。以此。天下多忌諱。而民彌貧。民多利器。國家滋昏。人多伎巧。奇物滋起。法令滋彰。盜賊多有。故聖人云。我無為而民自化。我好靜而民自正。我無事而民自富。我無欲而民自樸。

此所謂正治者，無爲也：無爲而於用兵，猶放任也，卽反謂以奇，是以知無爲而無不爲者，乃奇之又奇也。夫天下者，天下人之天下，非私也，如有事則私焉，不可以取天下。忌諱多者，有事焉而民彌貧。民多利器，多伎巧，彰法令，盜賊亦滋起矣。故聖人乃反之，民自化自樸矣。

五十七章 Chapter 57

Use the orthodox to govern a state;
Use the unorthodox to wage war.
Use non-involvement to win the world.
How do I know it is so?
By this.
The more restrictions and prohibitions there are,
the poorer the people become.
The sharper the people's weapons are,
the more national confusion increases.
The more skill artisans require,
the more bizarre (unorthodox) their products are.
The more precisely that laws are articulated,
the more thieves and outlaws increase.
Therefore the Sage says:
I practice Non-action
and the people are gradually transformed.
I love tranquility
and the people gradually become orthodox (upright).
I do not interfere
and the people gradually become wealthy.
I am without desires
and the people gradually return to simplicity.

Lecture: Orthodox government uses Non-action. War using Non-action is very casual, or in other words, unorthodox. It is evident from this that "through Non-action nothing is left undone" describes unorthodox unorthodoxy. As for the world, it belongs to the people; it is not private property. If a ruler interferes, it is for private ends. This is not the way to win the world. Too many restrictions and prohibitions interfere, and the people will become poorer and poorer. The more sharp weapons the people have, the more skilled as artisans they become, and the more precisely the laws are articulated, then the more thieves and outlaws will proliferate. Hence the Sage reverses the process so that the people will naturally be transformed and return to simplicity.

Chapter 58

五十八章

其政悶悶。其民淳淳。其政察察。其民缺缺。禍兮福之所倚。福兮禍之所伏。孰知其極。其無正。正復爲奇。善復爲妖。人之迷。其日固久。是以聖人方而不割。廉而不劌。直而不肆。光而不燿。

吾嘗謂老子之言，誠易知，愈解而愈不得明者，以人各以其意釋老子，故老子之化身千億，而老子愈神奇矣。譬如此節，焉用解乎？無已，以我意釋之，亦未必是老子意也。政無爲，烏可舉，猶悶悶然，缺缺，猶虧缺也。政者，正也，其無正，過乎察察，反而爲奇，是有爲也。且以奇爲妖，皆迷也，人恆以爲福，皆禍耳。不割而方，不劌而廉，言不待割而正也。不肆以直，不耀以光，其民淳淳然。

五十八章 Chapter 58

If the government is muffled and subdued,
The people will be simple and sincere.
If the government is strict and exacting,
The people will be lax and indifferent.
Good fortune depends on bad fortune.
Bad fortune lurks behind good fortune.
Who knows the ultimate end of this process?
If there is no orthodoxy,
The orthodox will return to the unorthodox.
Good becomes perverse.
The quandary of mankind has continued for a long time.
That is why the Sage makes square without cutting,
Squares corners without infringing,
Straightens without going to extremes,
Glows but does not glare.

Lecture: I often say that the words of Lao-tzu are easy to understand if one is sincere, yet the more they are interpreted, the less clear they become. Every person applies his own notions to Lao-tzu, thus transforming Lao-tzu into a thousand, a million different personalities, making him even more weird and mysterious. Take this chapter, for example. What need is there for an interpretation? Reluctantly, I add my own interpretation, fully realizing that it is not necessarily what Lao-tzu meant.

If the government practices Non-action, how can it accomplish anything? Thus it appears muffled and subdued. Laxity and indifference indicate deficiency. Proper government is orthodox. If the government is improper and becomes overbearingly strict and exacting, it becomes unorthodox, it acts for selfish motives. Moreover, the unorthodox leads to the unnatural, and the general quandary sets in. Under such circumstances, what people consider to be good fortune is completely bad. Not cutting yet making square nor infringing yet squaring corners means that incisive action is unnecessary to make things fitting and proper. Not going to extremes and yet straightening, not glaring and yet glowing will let the people be simple and sincere.

Chapter 59

五十九章

治人事天。莫若嗇。夫唯嗇。是謂早服。早服謂之重積德。重積德。則無不克。無不克。則莫知其極。莫知其極。可以有國。有國之母。可以長久。是謂深根固柢。長生久視之道。

七十章謂：吾言甚易知，甚易行。言有宗，事有君。正以人之不知，而不行也。如此節連續而自解之，倘仍不知，可不復也，嗇吝也。服習也。母，卽元牝，是爲衆妙之門。深固根柢以此，長生久視，亦不出乎此也。

五十九章 Chapter 59

In governing people and in serving heaven
nothing compares with frugality.
Frugality is "to acquire the habit early."
"To acquire the habit early" stresses accumulating Teh.
There is nothing which cannot be overcome, by stressing the accumulation of Teh.
If there is nothing which cannot be overcome,
Then one's limits are unfathomable.
If one's limits are unfathomable, he can rule a state.
If he can arrive at the Mother of the State, he can endure.
This is called "deeply rooted and firmly seated."
It is the Tao of longevity and lasting vision.

Lecture: Chapter 70 says, "my words are very easy to understand and very easy to practice . . . My words have their sources, my deeds their precedents." In fact, people do not try to understand and practice them. Lao-tzu continually repeats and explains himself. If people still do not understand his words, there is no use repeating them. "To acquire the habit early" is to practice at every opportunity. "Mother" means the Mysterious Female: it is the gateway to all wonders. To be "deeply rooted and firmly seated" in that place described as Mother, the Mysterious Female, is to have "longevity and lasting vision."

Chapter 60

六十章

治大國若烹小鮮。以道莅天下。其鬼不神。非其鬼不神。其神不傷人。非其神不傷人。聖人亦不傷人。夫兩不相傷。故德交歸焉。

老子雖主張小國寡民，却謂治大國若烹小鮮，此所謂無爲而無不爲。下文六十三與上三十四章，悉謂：聖人終不爲大，故能成其大。所謂：其鬼不神。及：聖人不傷人者，謂鬼不足以妨道，聖人視民如孩，臨國以道，毋用鋤其異己者，且以道治人，不但與人兩不相傷，且德亦交歸之焉。

六十章 Chapter 60

Ruling a large country is like cooking a small fish.
When the world is ruled from Tao, spirits do not haunt.
It is not that Spirits are no longer numinous,
But that their powers do not harm men.
It is not that their powers do not harm men,
The Sage also does not harm men.
If neither side harms the other,
Teh spreads throughout.

Lecture: Although Lao-tzu generally prefers a small state with a small population, here he says ruling a large state is like cooking a small fish. This is elsewhere described as "through Non-Action there is nothing that remains undone." Chapters 63 and 34 both state that the Sage never insists on his greatness, and so his greatness becomes a reality. This chapter says spirits do not haunt, and the Sage does not harm mankind; spirits cannot impede the Tao, and the Sage, regarding the people as his children and governing the country from Tao, refrains from weeding out (or "harming") those who do not agree with him. Moreover, in government according to Tao, not only do the two refrain from harming mankind, but also Teh spreads throughout all.

Chapter 61

六十一章

大國者下流。天下之交，天下之牝。牝常以靜勝牡。以靜爲下。故大國以下小國。則取小國。小國以下大國。則取大國。故或下以取。或下而取。大國不過欲兼畜人。小國不過欲入事人。夫兩者各得其所欲。大者宜爲下。

以國大比諸海，百川歸之，故謂下流。天下之交者，陰陽也，牝陰也，牝以常靜勝牡，此即易之所謂：天施而地受。總此章之主旨，取下之與陰，結尤謂：大者宜爲下，盖老氏以陰柔爲用也。

六十一章 Chapter 61

A great nation receives all that flows into it.
It is the place of intercourse with the world, the Feminine of the world.
The feminine always conquers the masculine through tranquility.
Tranquility is the lower position.
Hence, if a large country takes a position under a small country, it can win over the small country.
If a small country takes a position under a large country, it will win over the large country.
In the one case the large country purposely takes the lower position;
In the other case the small country simply remains in the lower position.
A large country wants no more than to protect its people and provide the environment for growth.
A small country wants no more than to enter into the service of a patron.
Thus, each party gets its wish.
It is fitting that the greater take the lower position.

Lecture: A large country is like a sea: all rivers flow into it. Therefore it "receives all that flows into it." "Intercourse with the world" refers to *yin* and *yang.* The Feminine is *yin* or the female principle. "The feminine always conquers the masculine through tranquility" is related to a line in the *Book of Change,* "heaven gives and the earth receives." Summing up, the text emphasizes the lower position and *yin,* especially in "it is fitting that the greater take the lower position." Thus does Lao-tzu discuss the use of *yin* and softness.

Chapter 62

六十二章

道者。萬物之奧。善人之寶。不善人之所保。美言可以市。尊行可以加人。人之不善。何棄之有。故立天子。置三公。雖有拱璧。以先駟馬。不如坐進此道。古之所以貴此道者。何不曰以求得。有罪以免邪。故爲天下貴。

道，猶萬物之奧藏，乃善人之寶貝也，不善人賴以保全之。美言可風行而成市，尊行人崇之，猶加於人也。不善何棄，見廿七章，聖人無棄人。立天子置三公，先之以寶璧，禮也。拱，捧也。然不如坐而進乎此道爲得也。意猶有進乎此者，古人何不曰：有罪可求得免？眞天下可貴之道也。

六十二章 Chapter 62

Tao is the enigma of all creation.
It is a treasure for the good man, a shelter for the bad.
Words of worth can create a city;
Noble deeds can elevate a man.
Even though a man is not good, how can he be abandoned?
A jade disc and a coach and four are presented to the emperor at his enthronement ceremony and to the Three Ministers at their installation,
But this cannot compare with riding toward the Tao.
Those ancients who prized Tao would instead have said,
"Seek and you will find,
Thus you will be freed from guilt."
Hence Tao is valued by the world.

Lecture: Tao is a mystery hidden in all things and a treasure for the good man. Men who are not good rely on it as a shelter. Words of worth can gain popularity and create a city. The people respect deeds; they can raise the man who does them above other men. How can a man, however bad, be abandoned? Chapter 27 states that the Sage abandons no one. During the enthronement of an emperor and during the installation of the Three Ministers, in accordance with ritual, first a precious jade disc is presented with two hands (out of respect), but this does not compare with riding onward to the Tao. Even more to the point, would not the ancients have said that finding the Tao frees one from guilt? Truly Tao is something the world should value.

Chapter 63

六十三章

爲無爲。事無事。味無味。大小多少。報怨以德。圖難於易。爲大於其細。天下難事。必作於易。天下大事。必作於細。是以聖人終不爲大。故能成其大。夫輕諾必寡信。多易必多難。是以聖人猶難之。故終無難矣。

爲無爲，事無事，猶無味之味也。不論怨之大小多少，報之以德，可參看四十九章。天下渾其心，聖人皆孩之，報怨以德者，亦渾其心己耳，可圖難於易，爲大於其細焉。反之者，輕諾寡信，多易反多難，必先之以難，反無難矣。

六十三章 Chapter 63

Act through Non-action.
Do without doing.
Taste the tasteless.
Great or small, many or few, repay injury with kindness (Teh).*
Plan to tackle the difficult when it is easy.
Undertake the great while it is small.
Begin the most difficult task in the world while it is still easy.
Begin the greatest task in the world while it is still small.
That is how the Sage becomes great without striving.
One who makes promises easily is inevitably unreliable.
One who thinks everything is easy inevitably finds everything difficult.
That is why the Sage alone regards everything as difficult and in the end finds no difficulty at all.

Lecture: Acting through Non-action and doing without doing are like tasting the tasteless. No matter whether your injuries are great or small, many or few, repay them with kindness (Teh).* In Chapter 49 the text says: ". . . his mind merges with the world. The Sage treats everyone as his children." Those who repay injury with kindness (Teh) are also merging their minds with the world. One must plan to tackle the difficult when it is easy and to undertake the great while it is still small, otherwise one will make light, unreliable promises or regard things as easy and thereby create difficulties. One must treat everything as difficult. Only then will there be no difficulty at all.

* *Translator's Note:* Here, where contrasted with "injury," the use of Teh has a more definite meaning, closer to "kindness."

六十四章 Chapter 64

When at peace, control is easy.
When there are no omens, planning is easy.
The brittle shatters easily.
The miniscule disperses easily.
Act before it is gone.
Establish order before confusion sets in.
A tree that takes several arm spans to circle grew from a tiny sprout.
A tower nine stories high began from a mound of earth.
A journey of a thousand *li* starts where the feet are.
To act consciously is to fail.
To clutch at is to lose.

Lecture: This paragraph advises acting before anything has happened and setting things in order before confusion arises. Do not think a mere sprout is not an omen. "A journey of a thousand *li* starts where the feet are" means that one can reach distance gradually and naturally. To act consciously and clutch at things is to court failure.

That is why the Sage does nothing and therefore fails at nothing,
Clutches at nothing and loses nothing.
The way people commonly handle affairs often leads to failure just at the point of success.
Be as cautious throughout as at the beginning, and there will be no failures.
That is why the Sage desires Non-desire.
He does not value rare things.
He studies the unfathomable.
He avoids the mistakes of ordinary people and assists all things to fulfill their natures, not daring to contrive any other action.

This paragraph does nothing more than expand on the meaning of the previous one. The desire of the Sage is not the desire of ordinary people. He does not study what ordinary people study. "He avoids the mistakes of ordinary people" means he avoids whatever the people mistakenly desire and mistakenly study; he simply assists all things to fulfill their natures, not daring to contrive any further action.

Chapter 64

。以輔萬物之自然。而不敢爲。

此節不過申前意耳，惟聖人之欲，乃非衆人之所欲也，學亦非衆人之所學也。復衆之所過者，謂復衆人所放任過去之欲與學也，是乃輔萬物之自然者，而不敢爲有爲也。

六十四章

其安易持。其未兆易謀。其脆易泮。其微易散。爲之於未有。治之於未亂。合抱之木。生於毫末。九層之臺。起於累土。千里之行。始於足下。爲者敗之。執者失之。

此節言爲之於未有，治之於未亂，毋以其毫末之未兆也。行千里者，始於足下，由邇而及遠，乃自然而然也。爲有爲，而執着者，敗之也。

是以聖人無爲。故無敗。無執。故無失。民之從事。常於幾成而敗之。愼終如始。則無敗事。是以聖人欲不欲。不貴難得之貨。學不學。復衆人之所過

Chapter 65

六十五章

古之善爲道者。非以明民。將以愚之。民之難治。以其智多。故以智治國。國之賊。不以智治國。國之福。知此兩者。亦稽式常。知稽式。是謂元德。元德深矣遠矣。與物反矣。然後乃至大順。

導之以愚，將以治多智。所謂反者，將以求其正。從極難，而終得最易。從大逆，而取其大順，此皆老氏之術也。賊，害也。稽，合也。式常，古之常式也。元德，見十章，重言之也。

六十五章 Chapter 65

The ancients who were most adept at ruling* did not try to enlighten the people,
But instead gradually made them stupid.
The people are difficult to govern because they are clever.
Hence, the nation's malefactor is one who uses cleverness to govern,
While the nation's benefactor is one who does not use cleverness to govern.
To understand both of those is also to harmonize with an eternal pattern.
To understand and harmonize with that pattern is called Profound Teh.
Profound Teh is so deep, so far-reaching,
It causes things to return and eventually reach Great Confluence.

Lecture: Guiding the people into ignorance will eventually control cleverness. This is "to return:" people will eventually seek out the orthodox path. Starting from the extremely difficult to finally reach the easiest and starting from Great Opposition to win over into Great Confluence are formulae of Lao-tzu. An "eternal pattern" is a model which has long held true. Chapter 10 explains Profound Teh. This chapter repeats the explanation.

* *Translator's Note:* Here Tao 道 is the same as tao 導, "to rule."

六十六章

江海所以能爲百谷王者。以其善下之。故能爲百谷王。是以欲上民。必以言下之。欲先民。必以言後之。是以聖人處上。而民不重。處前。而民不害。是以天下樂推而不厭。以其不爭。故天下莫能與之爭。

此節之意，以上言之熟矣，此亦老子之婆心，莫嫌其丁寧也，導之以愚，多智又將焉用。

六十六章 Chapter 66

The river and sea rule the hundred valleys by making the lower position an asset.
Hence, they are kings of the hundred valleys.
Therefore, if one desires to be over the people,
One must speak as if under them;
If one desires to be in front of the people,
One must speak as if behind them.
That is how the Sage remains over the people without oppressing them;
That is how he remains in front without blocking them.
The whole world is happy to draw near him and does not tire of him.
Because he does not compete,
Absolutely no one can compete with him.

Lecture: Lao-tzu has related the meaning of this chapter several times previously. This is just evidence of his compassionate heart. We should not reject him because he is repetitious. If we lead the people with ignorance, of what use will cleverness be?

Chapter 67

六十七章

天下皆謂我道大。似不肖。夫唯大。故似不肖。若肖。久矣。其細也。夫我有三寶。持而保之。一曰慈。二曰儉。三曰不敢爲天下先。慈故能勇。儉故能廣。不敢爲天下先。故能成器長。今舍慈且勇。舍儉且廣。舍後且先死矣。夫慈以戰則勝。以守則固。天將救之。以慈衞之。

大似不肖，跨竈也，是道也，何以嫌其大？三寶自釋已詳。違之者，取死之道也。不爭先，而成器長，亦上章所謂：大器晚成也。天將救之，因以其慈而衞之也。

六十七章 Chapter 67

All the world considers my Tao great and unrelated to anything else.
Precisely because it is so great it is "unrelated to anything else."
If it were related to other things, it would have grown small long ago.
I have three treasures which I possess and maintain securely.
The first is parental love.
The second is frugality.
The third is not daring to be first.
Possessing parental love, one can be courageous.
Possessing frugality, one can be generous.
Not daring to be first, one can lead all "instruments".
Today, many people reject parental love but desire courage,
They reject frugality but desire generosity,
And they reject following but desire to be first.
This is to court death.
Influenced by parental love, the offense will win wars, and the defense will be firm.
Through the influence of parental love, heaven will provide succor and protection.

Lecture: "Great and unrelated to anything else" means "the son surpasses the father*," and refers to the Tao. How can one reject the Tao for its greatness? The text explains "three treasures" clearly. To be contra-Tao chooses death. Refusing to compete for first and still becoming the leader of all "instruments" bears relation to an earlier line: "a great instrument is completed late." Heaven aids such a man. It protects him through the influence of its "parental love."

* *Translator's Note:* It should be pointed out that it is not a question of father and son relationship, but that the Tao surpasses all else.

Chapter 68

六十八章

善爲士者不武。善戰者不怒。善勝敵者不與。善用人者爲之下。是謂不爭之德。是謂用人之力。是謂配天古之極。

此節以上，亦已言之數矣。牝靜常勝牡，故或下以取，弱者，道之用，等語不與者，卽不爭不抗之意耳。配天古之極者，衆妙之門，玄牝也。

六十八章 Chapter 68

Good men are not aggressive.
A good fighter does not lose his temper.
Those skillful at overcoming an enemy never
confront him directly.
A skillful employer lowers himself.
This is the Teh of non-contention or strength from the ability
to use people.
It is in accord with most ancient heaven.

Lecture: This chapter also repeats what Lao-tzu has said several times before. The quiescence of the female always wins over the male, hence the lower position overcomes. Tao acts through softness. "Never confront (the enemy) directly" means to avoid wrangling or resisting. The Gate of all Mysteries—Mysterious Female—is "in accord with most ancient heaven."

Chapter 69

六十九章

用兵有言。吾不敢爲主。而爲客。不敢進寸而退尺。是謂行無行。攘無臂。扔無敵。執無兵。禍莫大於輕敵。輕敵幾喪吾寶。故抗兵相加。哀者勝矣。

此承上三寶之意。爲客，及退尺者，即不敢先也。執無兵，攘無臂，行等乎無行者，以退爲進也。扔，音仍，乃引之，不與抗而無敵，哀慈則勝，輕敵幾喪吾三寶矣。此亦老氏用兵之奇也。

六十九章 Chapter 69

Military tacticians have a saying:
"I dare not be the aggressor, but rather the defender;
I dare not advance an inch, but would rather retreat a foot."
This is to move without moving,
To raise one's fists without showing them,
To lead the enemy on but against no adversary,
To wield a weapon but not clash with the enemy's.
No disaster is greater than taking the enemy lightly.
If I take the enemy lightly, I am on the verge of losing my treasures.
Hence, when opposing troops resist each other,
The one stung by grief will be the victor.

Lecture: The text expands upon the "three treasures" mentioned previously, admonishing "(be) the defender" and "retreat a foot," following the precept "not daring to be first." To wield a weapon but not clash with the enemy's, to raise one's fists without showing them, and to move without moving mean that retreating is a way of advancing. To lead the enemy on without opposition is to be irresistible. Parental love, stung by grief, inspires victory. If I take the enemy lightly I am on the verge of losing my "three treasures." This is Lao-tzu's unorthodox military strategy.

Chapter 70

七十章

吾言甚易知。甚易行。天下莫能知。莫能行。言有宗。事有君。夫唯無知。是以不我知。知我者希。則我者貴。是以聖人被褐懷玉。

言有宗之一節，五十九章已舉而釋之。謂老氏之言，誠易知，惟說理，大異恒人，是以礙難行耳。夫唯無知句，可參閱二十章。我愚人之心也哉！我獨昏昏。故老氏從不尙知，是以人不之知。然知我者希，則我者貴，以聖人被褐懷玉，故知之者希也。

七十章 Chapter 70

My words are very easy to understand and very easy to practice.
Yet no one in the world can understand them;
No one can practice them.
My words have their sources, my deeds their precedents.
If people do not understand that, they do not understand me.
The fewer who know me, the more valuable I am.
That is why the Sage wears coarse clothes while carrying jade in his bosom.

Lecture: I have explained the section beginning "my words have their sources" in the Lecture on Chapter 59: Lao-tzu's teaching is truly easy to understand, but his definitions and logic are so different from the common man's that they are nearly impossible to practice. "People do not understand" is connected with Chapter 20: "what a fool's mind I have! . . . I alone want dullness and darkness." Because Lao-tzu never shows knowledge favor, people do not understand him. However, he says, "the fewer who know me, the more valuable I am." So the Sage "wears coarse clothes while carrying jade in his bosom," and very few people know about it.

Chapter 71

七十一章

知、不知、上。不知、知、病。夫唯病病。是以不病。聖人不病。以其病病。是以不病。

知、不知、上，五十六章：知者不言。猶若不知者，上也。不知、知、病，又有謂不知而言者，知其爲病也，是亦猶强不知以爲知之病耳。究老氏之言若是，惟其言簡耳。夫唯病病是以不病，蓋知其病之爲病，是以不病也，此聖人之所能也。

七十一章 Chapter 71

To know yet appear as not knowing is best.
To not know yet appear as knowing is sickness.
Whoever is sick of sickness will not be sick.
The Sage is never sick, because he is sick of sickness.
Thereby he is never sick.

Lecture: "To know yet appear as not knowing is best" harks back to Chapter 56: "one who knows does not speak," thereby appearing not to know. This is good. "To not know yet appear as knowing is sickness" describes one who does not know and yet speaks. His "knowledge" is his sickness, the disease of convincing oneself that he "knows" what he does not know. This is finally the real meaning of Lao-tzu's words, although they are very simple. "Whoever is sick of sickness will not be sick" means that one who recognizes this sickness as a disease will scrupulously avoid it. The Sage can do this.

Chapter 72

七十二章

民不畏威。則大威至。無狎其所居。無厭其所生。夫唯不厭。是以不厭。是以聖人自知不自見。自愛不自貴。故去彼取此。

不畏威，猶玩法也，必至加於大刑。無狎所居，警其居處，毋狎，欲其居敬也。無厭所生，以玩法至死，是猶厭其生耳。如不自厭，天下孰厭之者。是以聖人，自知自愛，可效法也。雖不自見自貴，乃去彼取此可耳。

七十二章 Chapter 72

If people do not fear the awesome, something more awful is imminent.
But do not be disrespectful of their dwellings;
Do not suppress their means of livelihood.
If not oppressed, they will not press.
That is why the Sage knows himself but does not reveal himself.
He has self-respect, but does not seek recognition.
Hence, he rejects one and takes the other.

Lecture: To have no fear of the awesome is the equivalent of trifling with the law and will inevitably result in more stringent punishments. "But do not be disrespectful of their dwellings," means to police their neighborhood and avoid rudeness in the desire to make their dwellings respectable. Trifling with the law until it becomes a matter of life-and-death suppresses the people's livelihood. On the other hand, if one is not strict with himself, who else will be? That is why the Sage with his self-knowledge and self-respect is able to study the laws of nature. Although he does not make a show of himself nor seek recognition, he is able to discriminate between "one" and "the other."

Chapter 73

七十三章

勇於敢則殺。勇於不敢則活。此兩者。或利或害。天之所惡。孰知其故。是以聖人猶難之。天之道不爭而善勝。不言而善應。不召而自來。禪然而善謀。天網恢恢。疏而不失。

此節雖繁複，以天網雖大，然疏而不失，若勇於不敢，則活。仍以守雌，合乎無爲之道。可見天道之難知，聖人則之，亦非易也。下文自不爭，不言，不召，至禪然善謀止，亦無爲而無不爲之意耳。禪者，靜也。

七十三章 Chapter 73

To have the courage to dare is to die.
To have the courage to dare not is to live.
Heaven abominates both these cases,
whether harmful or beneficial.
Who knows why?
Even the Sage feels it is difficult.
The Tao of heaven does not contend, yet it easily wins;
It does not speak, yet gets a good response;
It comes without being called;
It is calm, yet everything is minutely planned.
The web of heaven is so vast, so vast.
Though its mesh is wide, it loses nothing.

Lecture: This rather complicated chapter discusses the web of heaven. It is so vast, its meshed widely spaced, yet nothing is lost, just as those who have the courage to dare not, live. As always, this is related to cleaving to the Female and harmonizing with the way of Non-action. The Tao of heaven is difficult to understand. The Sage follows it even though it is not easy. What follows next in the text, from ". . . does not contend . . . speak . . . (nor is) called" to "it is calm, yet everything minutely planned," is simply a restatement of "Non-action, yet there is nothing left undone."

Chapter 74

七十四章

民不畏死。奈何以死懼之。若使民常畏死。而爲奇者。吾得執而殺之。孰敢。常有司殺者殺。夫代司殺者殺。是謂代大匠斲。夫代大匠斲者。希有不傷其手矣。

民若畏死，而爲奇異者，執而殺之，孰敢犯之。下文歎司殺者之未知用殺，代之者，不但非其分，亦不當行耳。

七十四章 Chapter 74

If the people do not fear death,
It is useless to scare them with the spectre of death.
If the people have a normal fear of death,
And some do something unorthodox,
Then I would catch them and put them to death.
Who would then dare to break the law?
There is always an executioner in charge of killing.
If someone tries to do the killing for the executioner,
It is called trying to chop wood for the Great Carpenter.
Few who substitute for the Great Carpenter do not injure their own limbs.

Lecture: If the people fear death, and some behave unorthodoxly and are caught and executed, who among the rest will dare oppose the social order? The remainder of the text bemoans the existence of the executioner. Not only is it inappropriate for anyone to substitute for the executioner, but it is also improper to be one.

Chapter 75

七十五章

民之饑。以其上食稅之多。是以饑。民之難治。以其上之有爲。是以難治。民之輕死。以其求生之厚。是以輕死。夫唯無以生爲者。是賢於貴生。

民之饑，以稅過重；民難治，以上之有爲所致；其輕死，以重視求生所驅使。反此，如上者若無爲，而使無以爲生者，是猶賢於貴生也。

七十五章 Chapter 75

If the people starve,
It is because those above them tax their livelihood too heavily.
That is why they starve.
If the people are unruly,
It is because those above them are too Active.
That is why they are unruly.
If the people take death lightly,
It is because they seek life's bounty.
That is why they take death lightly.
Those who live life without striving are exemplars of valuing life.

Lecture: The people starve because they are taxed too heavily. They are unruly because those above them have become selfish. The people take death lightly, because of the stress on the urgency of seeking life. Conversely, if those above practice Non-action, they allow the people to live naturally and so are worthy exemplars of valuing life.

Chapter 76

七十六章

人之生也柔弱。其死也堅强。萬物草木之生也柔脆。其死也枯槁。故堅强者死之徒。柔弱者生之徒。是以兵强則不勝。木强則兵。强大處下。柔弱處上。

堅强者，死之徒。柔弱者，生之徒。兵强則不勝，木强則兵。根强大，處下，枝條柔弱，處上，皆自然之理也。

七十六章 Chapter 76

When a person is born he is soft and supple.
When he dies he is stiff and hard.
All things, including plants, are soft and tender at birth.
At death they are withered and dry.
Hence the stiff and hard are the moribund ones;
The soft and supple are the vital ones.
That is why a strong army is not victorious.
A hardy tree gets the axe.
The hard and great are at the bottom.
The soft and supple are at the top.

Lecture: The stiff and hard are the moribund ones; the soft and supple are the vital ones. If an army is strong it will not be victorious; if a tree is hardy it gets the axe. The stiff and hard trunk is at the bottom, while the soft and supple branches are at the top. This is according to the laws of nature.

Chapter 77

七十七章

天之道。其猶張弓與。高者抑之。下者舉之。有餘者損之。不足者補之。天之道。損有餘。補不足。人之道則不然。損不足。以奉有餘。孰能有餘以奉天下。唯有道者。是以聖人爲而不恃。功成而不處。其不欲見賢。

張弓者，左支右抉，左手支持者，不得動，惟右抉者，可抑可舉也。有餘與不足，可以損與補者，命中進退之作用也。天之道，損有餘，而補不足；人則損不足，以奉有餘。孰能有餘以奉天下，唯有道者有是也。惟聖人與天地合德，爲而不恃，功成而不處，以其不欲以賢見也。

七十七章 Chapter 77

The Tao of heaven is like drawing a bow:
For high things, lower; for low things, raise;
If excessive, reduce; if insufficent, supplement.
The Tao of heaven reduces the excessive and supplements the insufficent.
The way of man is not so.
It takes from the insufficent and adds to the excessive.
Who can have enough surplus to supplement the world?
Only those with Tao.
That is why the Sage acts but does not demand subservience;
Is deserving of merit yet claims no credit.
He has no desire to show his worth.

Lecture: To draw a bow the left hand grips it and the right hand draws the string back. The left hand must be firm and unwavering. The right hand can raise or lower the arrow. If "excessive" or "insufficient" either "reduce" or "supplement" refers to tilting the bow forward or backward to bring the arrow in line with the bull's eye. The Tao of heaven reduces the excessive and supplements the insufficient, but man takes from the insufficient and adds to the excessive. Who can have enough surplus to supplement the world? Truly, only those who possess Tao. Only the Sage, in harmony with the Teh of heaven and earth, acts but does not demand subservience. He is deserving of merit yet claims no credit because he has no desire to advertise his worth.

Chapter 78

七十八章

天下莫柔弱於水。而攻堅强者。莫之能勝。其無以易之。弱之勝强。柔之勝剛。天下莫不知。莫能行。是以聖人云受國之垢。是謂社稷主。受國不祥。是爲天下王。正言若反。

水之攻堅强也，莫之與易，而天下雖知之，莫能行。故聖人云：受國之垢與不祥，方可爲社稷主，天下王。此正言若相反爾，亦猶知水之柔之爲用，而莫之行也。

七十八章 Chapter 78

Nothing in the world is softer and more supple than water,
Yet when attacking the hard and the strong,
nothing can surpass it.
The supple overcomes the hard.
The soft overcomes the strong.
None in the world do not know this.
Yet none can practice it.
That is why the Sage says to accept the filth of a nation
is to be the lord of the society.
To accept the disasters of a nation
is to be the ruler of the world.
Words of truth seem contradictory.

Lecture: In assaulting the hard and strong nothing is better than water, yet, though the whole world knows this, none can practice it. Hence the Sage says if one can accept even the filth and disasters of a nation, one will be lord of the society and ruler of the world. Words of truth seeming the exact opposite is similar to knowing the usefulness of the softness of water, yet not practicing it.

Chapter 79

七十九章

和大怨。必有餘怨。安可以爲善。是以聖人執左契。而不責於人。有德司契。無德司徹。天道無親。常與善人。

怨，猶惡也。善，猶恩也。恩怨之不可和，亦猶善惡之不可合也。是之謂和怨不足以爲善，聖人執契以待有德者，合也；無德者，徹之去耳。天道無私，惟與有德與善耳。

七十九章 Chapter 79

Compromising with great hatred inevitably leads to more hatred.
How can this be considered good?
That is why the Sage holds the left half of the tally-stick
yet does not demand others measure up.
To have Teh is to hold the other half of the tally-stick.
To be without Teh is to lose the tally-stick.
The Tao of heaven is not clannish.
It always dwells with the good man.

Lecture: Hatred is related to malice; goodness is related to kindness. As kindness cannot mix with hatred, goodness cannot harmonize with badness. Compromising with hatred is not worthy of the good. The Sage, holding the tally-stick, waits for the man with Teh to take the other half. This is harmonious. The man with no Teh loses hold of the stick and slips away. The Tao of heaven is without selfish preferences. It dwells only with the virtuous (Teh) and the good.

Chapter 80

八十章

小國寡民。使有什伯之器。而不用。使民重死。而不遠徙。雖有舟輿。無所乘之。雖有甲兵。無所陳之。使人復結繩而用之。甘其食。美其服。安其居。樂其俗。鄰國相望。雞犬之聲相聞。民至老死。不相往來。

此境在老子時，已是夢想中事。以至今日，朝夕間可往還於數萬里者，已成極端之反比例。若欲復結繩之用，除非天地有改造之時。什伯者，什夫伯夫之長。

八十章 Chapter 80

In a small country of few people, even if there are hundreds of weapons, they are unnecessary.
Cause the people to respect death and they will not migrate.
Though there are ships and vehicles, no one boards them.
Though there are armor and weapons, no one parades with them.
Let men return to knotting strings and using them.
Food will be sweet.
Clothes will be beautiful.
Homes will be comfortable.
Customs will delight.
Although neighboring states will see each other and hear the other's chickens and dogs,
The citizens of each will age and die without establishing contact with the other.

Lecture: Such conditions were a dream even during Lao-tzu's time. Today, when it is possible to travel tens of thousands of miles between dawn and dusk, this eventuality is out of the question. If we wanted to return to knotting ropes, we would have to start the world from primitive beginnings again.

Chapter 81

八十一章

信言不美。美言不信。善者不辯。辯者不善。知者不博。博者不知。聖人不積。既以爲人已愈有。既以與人已愈多。天之道。利而不害。聖人之道。爲而不爭。

此老子之眞、善、美，有眞而後有善，有善而後有美，被褐懷玉，美在其中，非天下所皆知也。知者不博，精一也。己以爲人，己以與人，愈有而愈多，是聖人法天之施爲，故不積耳。且天之道，遂其生長，而不害；聖人法之，故爲而不爭。

八十一章 Chapter 81

Words of truth are not beautiful;
Beautiful words are not truthful.
The good do not argue;
Those who argue are not good.
The wise are not extensively learned;
The extensively learned are not wise.
The Sage is not mean.
Simply doing things for others he feels greater fulfillment.
Simply giving to others he feels he has gained more.
The Tao of heaven benefits and does not harm.
The Tao of the Sage is to accomplish without competing.

Lecture: Herein is Lao-tzu's idea of truth, goodness, and beauty. One must be truthful to be good and be good to have beauty. Dress in coarse clothes and carry the jade in one's bosom; beauty is within. It is not something that everyone in the world can know. "The wise are not extensively learned" means to concentrate on the One. Doing things for others and giving himself, the Sage feels fulfillment and gain; the Sage follows the example of heaven and is not mean. Moreover, the Tao of heaven promotes birth and growth rather than harm. The Sage follows Tao, hence he accomplishes without competing.

附錄道德論 Appended Remarks on Tao and Teh

Tao has three elements, which the *Book of Change* describes as founding heaven, founding earth, and founding mankind. Teh can no more be separated from Tao than heaven from earth, *yin* fron *yang,* or, among humans, man from woman or husband from wife. That is why the *Great Learning* and the *Doctrine of the Mean* open with words about Tao and Teh.

In simple words, that heaven aids in the creation of life is Tao; that earth aids in birth and growth is Teh. If one believes humanism and justice are sufficient to comprise Tao and Teh, one denies heaven and earth and ruins the Three Agencies (*san-ts'ai*: heaven, earth, and mankind). If one denies heaven and earth and yet speaks of *An Inquiry On The Tao* (an essay by Han Yu, 768-824 A.D.), then people must say, "what (Han Yu) calls 'Tao' is not the true Tao; what he calls 'Teh' is not the true Teh," rather it would be the Tao and Teh of non-heaven and non-earth.[1]

How can one forget the words of Confucius in the Commentary on the *Book of Change?* From them I know the words of Han Yu are too simple. He did not think profoundly enough. I have nothing to say about his debunking the followers of Lao-tzu and defending the Tao of mankind.

What Lao-tzu calls Tao and Teh is far from realization. Even in his own time, Lao-tzu himself knew that he could not implement his Tao, and so he left. The Han Dynasty believed in government through Non-action and held the Yellow Emperor in highest reverence, but they were unable to govern as if China were a small state with an ignorant populace.

Since it is obvious that the Tao and Teh of Lao-tzu has long since become "the private utterance of one man,"[2] what is the use of raising such a storm of protest? Mencius rebutted Yang Chu and Mo Ti because he wanted to implement humanism *(jen)* and justice *(yi).* I do not know what Han Yu wanted to implement when he rebutted Lao-tzu.

"Alas! The Tao has not been implemented for a long time." Those who want to implement a system, whether it be Tao and

Teh or humanism and justice, must have someone with the virtues of Confucius or Mencius to lead them, or they will fail. During Confucius' lifetime he had 3,000 disciples. Those who came after took his Tao to the public, and even when their audience was ten or one hundred or even one thousand times as many, actual believers were few. However, Confucius said, "the most wise and the most stupid do not change," so how could everyone belong to the school of Confucius? One may despise the unproductiveness of Buddhists and Taoists among the "six consumers of grain,"[3] yet even if one did not follow Lao-tzu or Buddha, he would not necessarily be involved in production. Although one may diminish the effects of calamities, they are probably unavoidable.

Now, to establish Tao and Teh and humanism and justice, government and education must be unified. Of what use is it to prevent people from becoming Taoist or Buddhist? The desires of people today are overflowing and morality is almost nil. If there are people who wish to follow Lao-tzu or Buddha and who have not completely lost their moral awareness, why scold them?

Confucius was a man, Mencius was a man, I also am a man. Why can I not expand myself to the further reaches of mankind? If I can improve people's lives, need I despair or mourn over those who have fallen from the human level? If I did despair, even though I had Confucius and Mencius as my father and brother, what use would their teachings be?

I have written this discussion of Tao and Teh to encourage people to respect the powers that be (that which supports them—the earth— and covers them—heaven) and not bring their own births to shame. If it were not for the leadership of Confucius and Mencius who showed us how to stand as human beings, what would have happened to those who came after them? If there had only been one or two people somewhere in the wide world who could shoulder the responsibility, then even though the sky shuddered, there would have been someone to hold it up. Why fear that people will not follow me? And why insist that every single person practice the Tao of Confucius and Mencius?

The 2nd day of the 3rd moon, 1968
Whiskers Man Cheng of Yung-chia
On sojourn in New York

Translator's Notes:

1. Professor Cheng is using Han Yu's words debunking Lao-tzu to refute Han Yu's line of reasoning about Tao and Teh.

2. A quote from Han Yu's *An Inquiry On The Tao (Yuan Tao)*: "What (Lao-tzu) called the Way was only the Way as he understood it and not what I call the Way. What he called virtue was only the virtue as he understood it and not what I call virtue . . . What Lao-tzu called the Way and virtue (Tao and Teh) was devoid of humanity and righteousness (*jen* and *yi,* the basic principles of Confucius), which was the private opinion of one man." *A Source Book in Chinese Philosophy,* by Wing-tsit Chan, Princeton University Press, p. 454.

3. Again a quote from Han Yu's *An Inquiry On The Tao.* Han Yu argues that Taoists and Buddhists constitute one of six classes of society that consume grain (food) but the Taoists and Buddhists do not produce anything themselves. Therefore they are mere leeches on society's bounty and ought to be put to work instead of sitting in monasteries.

說，非一政教不可，徒欲阻人之不入老與佛，將焉益哉？今者人慾橫流，天理幾滅，其有欲歸老與佛者，而其天良尚未喪盡，何備責焉。仲尼，人也，孟軻，人也，我亦人也，我何以不能推己及人，與人爲善，寧自暴棄，喪失人格者乎？若是，雖父兄如孔孟，教之何裨？我之作道德論者，欲儘人敬其覆載，無忝所生，苟無孔孟之倡，立人之道，寧後人乎？天地之間，能有一二人任其責，天之欲圮，可以揩之，何懼人之不我從也？又何必盡天下人，皆行孔孟之道者焉？

戊申三月初二永嘉鄭　曼髯客紐約

誠爲遠而。當其時，聃亦自知道之不行，去之。漢雖欲無爲爲治，崇尚黃帝已耳。未然從愚民小國之政。可見聃之所謂道德，早已成一人之言，何用大聲疾呼而闢之？孟軻之闢楊墨，以其欲行仁義也，愈之闢老，未知其欲何行也。嗚呼！道之不行久矣，必欲行道德仁義之說者，非有孔孟之德行者倡之，不行也。及仲尼之身，弟子三千。後之宗者，盛行其道，十倍或百倍，甚至千倍，其信徒有限耳。且仲尼謂上智與下愚不移，又何能盡列於孔氏之門？倘惡食粟之家六，其不歸老與佛者，亦未必資生事焉，減輕禍害，或亦不免。然欲建樹道德仁義之

附錄道德論

夫道有三，易謂立天立地立人耳。德者不可離乎道，猶天之與地，陰之與陽，人之有男女與夫婦也。故學庸首言道德者，以是。簡言之，天之資始，道也；地之資生，德也。若合仁義，而始足爲道德者，則離乎天地，隳三才也。離天地而謂原道，人亦必謂道爾所道，非其所謂道也；德爾所德，非其所謂德也。是之謂無天無地之道德也。易繫孔子之言，何可忘也？吾以是知韓愈之言之易，不思之甚；惟闢老者，維護人道，吾無間焉。老聃之謂道德。

Brief Biography of Professor M.C. Cheng

Man-ch'ing Cheng was born in Chekiang Province in the *fu* of Yung-chia (present-day Wen-chou) in 1901 on the 25th day of the 6th moon (Chinese calendar).

His father died when Cheng was a small child, and his widowed mother taught him poetry and calligraphy. He was said to possess a photographic memory and had already memorized the Confucian classics when, at age nine, a brick fell from a rotten wall severely fracturing his skull. For two days and nights he lay as if dead. Then a teacher of martial arts came by, examined the boy and said that he was not dead. The man went to the mountains and gathered herbs which brought the boy back to consciousness. However, young Cheng had completely lost his memory and was like a vegetable.

At age 10 friends and relations sent him to apprentice with a painting master, Wang Hsiang-ch'an. The youngster could do little more than set out paper and grind ink. After about 4 years of this, master Wang's wife asked the teenager to do a painting. He declined, saying he had never done one. After gentle but firm encouragement he took up his master's brush and painted a flowering wisteria. His teacher was astounded, because the painting was not only marvelously good, it was in a style refreshingly unfamiliar to him.

When Cheng entered his master's studio the following morning to prepare paper and ink for the day, he found his painting on the table with an inscription by his teacher proclaiming Cheng a painter in his own right and describing how much his work should sell for. From that time on (age 14), Cheng supported his family by painting.

The next few years he spent in Hangchou in the company of a circle of literati, developing his painting, poetry, and calligraphy.

At age 18 he went to Peking and soon was invited to teach poetry at Yu-wen University.

In his mid-twenties, Cheng was invited to be director of the department of Chinese painting at the Shanghai School of Fine Arts.

During his mid- to late-twenties, several important things happened to Cheng. Due to inhaling so much chalk dust while teaching, he developed third-degree tuberculosis and was pronounced incurable by doctors. At this time, a friend introduced him to Yang Ch'eng-p'u, the renowned grand-master of T'ai-chi Ch'uan. Within half a year, the fever had subsided, he no longer coughed blood, and soon the coughing ceased altogether. Cheng maintained his practice of T'ai-chi Ch'uan all his life and became an internationally renowned master himself.

In his late-twenties he helped found the College of Chinese Culture and Art in Shanghai, of which he was vice president.

He also met Sung You-an of Anhui Province, whose family had been famous for nine generations as practitioners of traditional Chinese medicine. During summers and school vacations, Cheng studied medicine with the elderly doctor, plumbing the depths of the Tao of medicine. In later years, Cheng and others founded the National Chinese Medical Association, which, for the first time in Chinese history, succeeded in uniting all the famous doctors of traditional Chinese medicine on the mainland. Cheng was elected its president. In 1946, he took a position on the National Assembly for the Construction of the Constitution of the Republic of China. The following year he was elected to the National Assembly as the representative of the community of doctors of Chinese medicine, a position he held until his death in 1975.

But to return to his earlier history, at age 30 he retired from teaching and travelled to Yang-hu in Kiangsu Province and studied with master of classics Ch'ien Ming-shan. For three years he "burned the midnight oil" studying the classics and the sages until he finally "entered the Tao of knowledge."

As a result, his poetry became pure, clear, robust and real. His calligraphy was full, unified, even and solid. The strength of his brush stroke seemed to penetrate through the paper. His painting was simple yet refined, and at the same time weighty.

At age 40, Cheng married Miss Yi-tu Ting. Their children number five in all: three girls and two boys.

Professor Cheng had five especially strong points: poetry, painting, calligraphy, traditional Chinese medicine, and T'ai-chi Ch'uan. Furthermore, he could unify them as if they were pearls threaded on a single string. That string was the Tao.

Because he studied deeply the classics and the sages, he fathomed the depths and the principles of philosophy. Thus the past and the present, the sages of old and this man of the modern world reached a harmony. The venerable Yü Yu-jen praised him in this way, "he is a unique talent of this era. What others regard as the most difficult of matters, he alone does easily and well."

Cheng left mainland China in 1949 and relocated in Taipei, Taiwan. He and such luminaries as Yü Yu-jen, Ch'en Han-kuang, Chang Chao-ch'in and others formed a poetry society. With another group of people he formed the Seven Friends of Painting and Calligraphy. He was also among those who began the Republic of China Fine Arts Society. He was invited to a life-time professorship at the College of Chinese Culture, and was named Director of Fine Arts of the American branch of the Republic of China Cultural Renaissance Movement.

During the 25 years after leaving mainland China, Cheng had many one-man shows both in Taiwan and abroad. Among those, one was at the National Cernuschi Gallery in Paris and another was at the 1964 World's Fair in New York, a third was at the FAR Gallery in 1968, and a fourth was at the Hudson River Musuem in 1973.

Cheng also established the Shr Jung School of T'ai-chi Ch'uan in Taipei. When he went to America, he continued teaching T'ai-chi. In fact, this traditional Chinese martial art proved to be a bridge between Eastern and Western culture. Professor Cheng's profound understanding of Chinese philosophy enabled him to show the relationship between T'ai-chi Ch'uan and the teachings of the Chinese sages.

Both in Taiwan and America he gave lecture-demonstrations on painting and calligraphy. He also taught classes on Lao-tzu's *Tao Teh Ching*, and Confucius' *Doctrine of the Mean, Great Learning*, and the *Analects*.

Professor Cheng first visited New York in January 1964, where I first met him. I studied with him from then on, eventually becoming fluent enough in Chinese to act as interpreter and American secretary. I was with him when he passed away on March 26, 1975, in Taipei.

A brief description of his publications includes several volumes of poetry, including a commentary on poems of the T'ang Dynasty, several volumes of paintings and calligraphy, plus a volume on the theory and principles of poetry, calligraphy, and painting, several volumes on traditional Chinese medicine, several volumes on T'ai-chi Ch'uan, two of them in English, two motion pictures on T'ai-chi Ch'uan, both in English, commentaries on Lao-tzu and on the Confucian classics, including the *Great Learning,* the *Doctrine of the Mean,* the *Analects,* and the *Book of Change.* Plus, two original works on philosophy, culture, and self-cultivation.

The accomplishments of his lifetime were all directed toward developing and expanding Chinese culture.

Tam Gibbs